THE GOOSE'S GOLD
金鹅号的宝藏

[美] 罗恩·罗伊 著
[美] 约翰·史蒂文·格尼 绘 叶雯熙 译

人物介绍

丁丁

三人小组的成员,聪明勇敢,喜欢读推理小说,紧急关头总能保持头脑冷静。喜欢在做事之前好好思考!

三人小组的成员,活泼机智,喜欢吃好吃的食物,常常有意想不到的点子。

乔希

露丝

三人小组的成员,活泼开朗,喜欢从头到脚穿同一种颜色的衣服,总是那个能找到大部分线索的人。

哈撒韦奶奶

露丝的奶奶,一个健康、时髦的老人。差点被卷入金钱诈骗的案件中,幸亏孩子们成功识破嫌疑人的诡计,没有造成损失。

自称是发现了宝藏的淘金人,想让哈撒韦奶奶在内的老年人投资他们的寻宝行动。

斯派克

奇普

自称是发现了宝藏的淘金人,想让哈撒韦奶奶在内的老年人投资他们的寻宝行动。

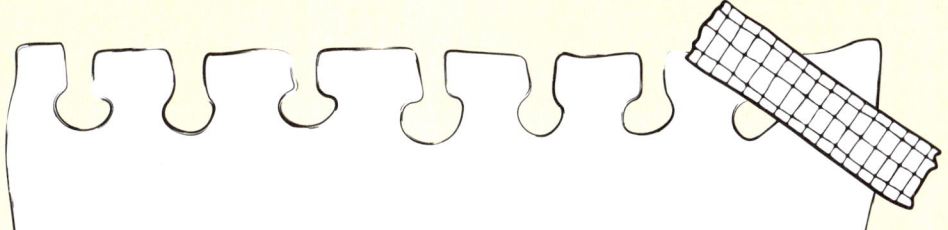

字母 G 代表 greed，贪婪……

斯派克和奇普搬着装满金子的箱子走了出来，哈撒韦奶奶跟着他们走到了门廊处。

"谢谢您给我们叫出租车，哈撒韦太太。"斯派克说，"您真的认为您的朋友会帮助我们吗？"

哈撒韦奶奶微笑着说："我毫不怀疑。我周一早上就和我的银行经理说这件事！"

一辆黄色的出租车靠边停了下来，斯派克和奇普带着箱子上了车。出租车开动了，他们向窗外挥手致意。

…………

"如果我马上就要发财了，我也会很兴奋。"乔希说。

丁丁站了起来。"我不认为她马上就要发财了。"他说，"我觉得她马上就要被劫财了！"

第一章

"嘿，妈妈，我已经到佛罗里达州啦！"丁丁对着电话那头说。他透过机场的大窗子向外看了一眼，继续说道："我这里可以看到棕榈树！气温有27摄氏度！"

丁丁的全名是唐纳德·戴维·邓肯，朋友们都叫他丁丁。学校正在放寒假，他和乔希、露丝准备去拜访哈撒韦奶奶。她住在一个叫基韦斯特的岛上。

丁丁的妈妈祝他玩得开心，并叮嘱他"要注意礼节"。

丁丁对着电话咧嘴笑了笑。"注意什么礼节？嘿嘿，和您开玩笑呢，妈妈！过几天见。"

他挂了电话，弯下身子，拿起自己的背包时，旁边电话亭里的一双脚闯入他的视线。这双脚很黑，穿着一双凉鞋，毛茸茸的脚脖子上有一个文身，图案是一个鹰头。

丁丁听到了这个男人说话的声音。他正小声说："……然后我们拿上票子一分。他们这辈子也别想找到我们！"

"拿上票子一分？这家伙正蓄谋抢劫吗？"丁丁想。

他探过身去，凑近那个电话亭，想听得更清楚些。

"这些老家伙的腰包鼓鼓的。"他轻声说，"我们一进一出，再把鹅淹死，然后就人间蒸发！"

丁丁眨了眨眼睛，心想：老家伙的腰包鼓鼓

的？把鹅淹死？到底怎么回事？

突然，乔希在丁丁面前打了一个响指。"呼叫丁丁。"他说。

"走啦，我们要去找我奶奶了。"露丝说。

丁丁离开公用电话亭，瞥了一眼旁边的位置，但是里面已空无一人。

他快跑着跟上了乔希和露丝。

"伙计们，你们一定不会相信我刚刚听到了什么！"他说，"我想有人正在策划一场抢劫！"

乔希和露丝看着丁丁。"你在开玩笑吗？"露丝问。

"没有，我是说真的！"丁丁说。

丁丁努力模仿了那个男人小声说话的样子："他说：'拿上票子，把鹅淹死！'"

乔希看着他的这位朋友："就这些？"

丁丁点点头："嗯，他还说了一些关于腰包鼓鼓的老人的话。"

"也许他说的是'把面团[1]烤[2]上,把鹅烤至金黄[3]。'"露丝说,"听起来像是一位厨师,不是抢劫犯。"

突然,他们听到有人在叫他们:"哟,孩子们,这里!"

"她来啦!"露丝激动地说,"嘿,奶奶!"

孩子们飞快走向一位满头白发、面带微笑的老人。

"亲爱的,看看你都长多大啦!"哈撒韦奶奶抱了抱露丝,继续说,"圣诞快乐!"

露丝脸红了:"谢谢奶奶。这是我最好的朋友,丁丁和乔希。朋友们,这是我的哈撒韦奶奶!"

哈撒韦奶奶身材矮小,肤色黝黑,穿着一条短裤和一件紫色的T恤衫,还反戴着一顶棒

---

1. 原文 dough,既表示"生面团",在俚语当中又表示"钱,票子"。——译者
2. 原文 bake "烤",与前文丁丁所听到的 take "拿"发音相近,因此便产生了歧义。——译者
3. 原文 brown "把食物烤至金黄",与前文丁丁所听到的 drown "淹没"发音相近,因此便产生了歧义。——译者

球帽!

奶奶和小伙子们握了握手。"我听说过你们俩,"她说,"行李都拿到了吧?让我们回去好好享用一顿丰盛的晚餐。"

哈撒韦奶奶带着他们走出机场。这里的夜晚闷热潮湿,每个人都穿着短裤和凉鞋。

"朋友们,家里的雪都有一英尺[1]高了!"乔希说,"我等不及要看看大海啦!"

"我家不远处就有一个美丽的海滩。"哈撒韦奶奶说,"12月的海水十分温暖,我想你们马上就会感受到的。"

孩子们挤进了她的白色小车。"系上安全带,孩子们。"她说。

丁丁和乔希爬到车的后座。丁丁差点一屁股坐到一双轮滑鞋上。"把它们放在车厢地板上就行。"奶奶说。

乔希朝丁丁使了个眼色,然后问哈撒韦奶奶:"您会玩轮滑吗?"

1.英美制长度单位。1英尺=0.3048米。——编者

她透过后视镜向乔希挤了挤眼睛,说:"周二和周五的时候会玩。剩下的时间我会去慢跑或者游泳!"

金鹅号的宝藏

　　不一会儿,他们嗖地从一条繁华的街道驶过。丁丁望着窗外闪过的棕榈树,穿过一排排整齐的房屋,瞥见了蓝色的海洋和几乎纯白的

海滩。

"看！一只鹈鹕！"乔希指着窗外喊道。

"你在这里能看到很多这种鸟。"哈撒韦奶奶说，"它们不怕人。我曾经看到过一只鹈鹕俯冲下来，抢走了一个女孩的冰激凌甜筒！"

"它们休想在我这儿来这一套！"乔希说。

"我们到咯！"哈撒韦奶奶说道。她把车驶进了一条停车道，车道两旁蔷薇环绕。

丁丁看到一栋粉色的小房子，窗子是蓝色的。窗台上的花盆里栽满了色彩鲜艳的花朵。门前的台阶上种着粉色的天竺葵。

"您的房子真漂亮，哈撒韦夫人！"乔希说。

她笑了笑："叫我奶奶就好。谢谢你的夸奖！"

孩子们跟着哈撒韦奶奶进入黄色的客厅。客厅的角落里放着一张桌子，桌子上立着一棵圣诞树。

"好啦，放下你们的行李，吃点东西吧！"

哈撒韦奶奶带着露丝和乔希进了厨房。"希望你们喜欢吃炸鸡块！"

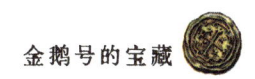

丁丁慢吞吞地跟在后面。他一直在想打电话的那个人。

他想,如果那个人只是在谈论食物,为什么要偷偷摸摸地说呢?

第二章

"我闻到了饼干的味道。"第二天一早,乔希说。

丁丁翻过身看向乔希。乔希正坐在床上,用自己的鼻子嗅来嗅去。

丁丁咧嘴笑了:"你看起来像一只兔子,乔希。"

"不,我没开玩笑,"乔希走到床边,用鼻子深深一吸,"没错,是饼干。还加了巧克力豆!"

门口传来敲门声。"快一点，伙计们！"露丝说，"奶奶在做早餐啦！"

丁丁和乔希急匆匆地穿上了短裤和T恤衫。快速洗漱完，他们匆匆下了楼。

哈撒韦奶奶站在火炉旁，用勺子将煎饼糊舀在热烤盘上。她穿戴着跑步的装备，头发用红色的头绳扎了起来。"早上好，小伙子们。睡得怎么样？"她说。

"很好。"丁丁说，"就是乔希一整晚都在打呼噜。"

"哈！"露丝一边笑，一边将橙汁倒进四个玻璃杯。露丝喜欢全身都穿同一种颜色，今天她穿了一条绿色的短裤、一件绿色的T恤衫，还有一双绿色的果冻鞋。

乔希瞥了一眼灶台。"我觉得我闻到了巧克力饼干的味道。"

哈撒韦奶奶微笑着说："小伙子很敏锐哟！烤箱里有一批饼干，马上就能出炉啦。"

乔希用手肘推了推丁丁。"我说得没错吧？我很敏锐的！"

奶奶把一盘煎饼端上桌："我在给我的伙伴做饼干。"

"您的伙伴是谁啊，奶奶？"露丝问。

奶奶神秘地笑了笑，说："这是一个惊喜。你们可以期待一下。"

吃早餐时，奶奶跟孩子们介绍了在岛上可以看到的风景。

"一定要搭老城电车。"她说，"它能带你们把城里逛个遍。"

"我们要怎么去海滩呢？"乔希问道。

"走到街道的尽头，然后向右转，再经过两个街区，你就能看到大海啦。"哈撒韦奶奶回答。

"需要我们帮您打扫卫生吗？"露丝问。

"我跑完步会自己打扫的。"哈撒韦奶奶回答道，"祝你们玩得开心，午餐的时候我们再见。"

孩子们每人拿上一块刚出炉的饼干，就迫不及待地出门去了。

10分钟后，他们就拎着运动鞋在海滩上蹚水了。

海滩上，丁丁留意着别人的脚，他看见很

多人的脚脖子上有文身,但没有谁的文身图案是老鹰。

他们走了几步,从海滩来到一条宽阔的混凝土长堤,这儿摆了椅子和桌子,小贩们在贩卖食物和纪念品。一个男人正用橘子和葡萄柚玩杂耍,灰色的大鹈鹕立在柱子上,正等着游客来给它们喂食。

"我们去看看那些船吧!"乔希指着长长的木质码头提议。

孩子们奔跑着穿过长堤,到达了码头。丁丁看见了一个指示牌,上面写着:小心碎片和鱼钩!禁止赤脚!

垂钓者排成一排。一个小女孩大叫一声,拉起鱼竿,钓起了一条有丁丁手臂大小的银鱼。

孩子们穿上鞋子,漫步在长长的码头上。船只一艘贴着一艘,停靠在码头两侧的泊位。

目之所及,人们都在给他们的船进行清洗、抛光或者刷漆。

"我希望我能有一艘船。"乔希一边说,一边沿着码头继续向前走,"我可以在船上生活,然

后周游世界。"

"我和丁丁呢?"露丝问。

"哦,我会雇你来做我的厨师。"乔希对露丝说,"你可以给我做饼干和比萨。"

他又用屁股撞了一下丁丁,说:"丁丁可以帮我洗衣服,整理床铺!"

"是的,对。"丁丁说,"我还能炒你的鱿鱼呢!"

"听!我听到了音乐声!"乔希说。

码头的尽头有一台收音机,收音机旁边站着一个人,正拿着画笔,在一艘白色小船的船舷上画着金色的花体字母。他刚刚画完字母 G 和 O。

那人的手指被晒得黝黑,上面沾满了金色的油漆。他个子矮小,但手臂上的肌肉健壮,看起来像个举重运动员。

还有一个男人站在他旁边吃着松饼。这个男人又高又瘦,金色的头发被扎成马尾辫。他们两个都穿着宽松的牛仔裤和吊带背心。

瘦高的男人朝孩子们点点头。"你们好。"他说。

"我喜欢你们的船。"乔希说,"你们住在船上吗?"

瘦高的男人调小了收音机的音量。"船的前部有两张床。"他说,"还有一间厨房和一间浴室。"

丁丁看到船的一侧拴着一条黄色小皮艇,两根长长的钓竿被放在甲板上。

"那是钓鱼船吗?"丁丁问。

他摇摇头,说:"不是,我们在寻宝,潜到水里找金子。"

"真的吗?"乔希说,"那也太酷了!"

这个男人用拿着松饼的手朝大海挥了挥。"那儿有很多沉船,"他咧着嘴笑道,"我和斯派克就发现了一艘。"

那个拿着画笔的人狠狠地瞪了他的朋友一眼,说:"奇普,也许这些孩子对我们的事情不感兴趣。"

奇普耸耸肩。"只是表示一下友好嘛。"

斯派克继续描字。

"你们找到金子了吗?"乔希问。

奇普看了看斯派克。

A to Z 神秘案件

"是的,我们找到了一些。"斯派克回答道。

"可以给我们看看吗?"露丝问。

斯派克思索了一会儿,然后将他的画笔递给奇普。"当然。"他说,"上船来吧,小心脚。"

斯派克从楼梯下到船舱。回来的时候,他的

手里拿着一些闪闪发光的东西。

"这些是西班牙硬币。"斯派克告诉孩子们,"差不多有四百年了。"

孩子们紧紧地盯着斯派克手中的金币。

"漂亮吧?"他问。

这些大大的金币在太阳下闪闪发光。

"太令人惊叹了!"乔希说道。

第三章

孩子们谢过斯派克和奇普后,便沿着码头往回走。

"我想知道这些金币值多少钱。"乔希说道。

"值很多钱!"露丝说。

乔希感叹道:"潜水寻宝很酷,对吧?"

"乔希,"丁丁说,"你需要了解使用氧气罐和其他装备的方法。他们可需要潜到很深的海底!"

这时,街对面驶来一辆橙色电车,乘客们正在排队上车。

"电车来了!"露丝说,"我们快上车!"

孩子们冲了过去。他们爬上车,在司机的正后方坐定。当车里差不多坐满后,电车猛地一晃,沿着街道向前驶去。

"电车这是要开往哪里?"丁丁问司机。

"我们哪里都去,小伙子!"司机说着,递给丁丁一张地图,"看到那些蓝色的圆圈了吗?那是我们的停靠站点。你们可以在任意站点下车,我开车绕回来的时候,你们也可以再上来。"

司机在一座白色建筑前停了车。这里摆满了花箱,里面盛开着鲜花。建筑物前的指示牌上写着:梅尔·费希尔的博物馆——你将在此领略西班牙金银财宝的风采。

"梅尔·费希尔是谁?"丁丁问司机。

"梅尔·费希尔发现了一艘装满金银的西班牙旧船。"他说,"他发现的部分东西就陈列在这座博物馆里。"

A to Z 神秘案件

他指着指示牌，说道："为什么不下车去看看呢？我大约 45 分钟后会绕回来。"

"好！"乔希说。

孩子们下了电车，跟随着其他参观者进了博物馆。

里面是一排排的玻璃展柜，每个展柜里都陈列着闪闪发光的金银珠宝。

孩子们一边走，一边欣赏着这些无价之宝。

过了一会儿，露丝在梅尔·费希尔的照片前停了下来。照片里他戴着一条长长的金项链。这条金链就放在照片下面的一个展柜里。

"看！"露丝说，"这条纯金项链是 1622 年制

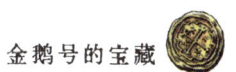
金鹅号的宝藏

造的,重200磅[1],价值超过一百万美元!"

"伙计们,想象一下你脖子上戴着那条项链的场景,那得是什么感觉!"乔希说。

---

1. 英美制质量或重量单位。1磅=0.4536千克。——编者

丁丁仔细端详着一张照片，照片里是梅尔·费希尔的船。"瞧，上面说他差不多花了20年才找到宝藏！"他说。

"既然谈到了食物，我们不如去吃午餐吧。"乔希说。

"我们可没在谈论食物。"露丝说。

"好吧，但是我的肚子空空如也。"乔希说，"看这些宝藏让我饿得慌！"

几分钟后，电车又到了博物馆。

"你们觉得那些金子怎么样？"司机问他们，"令人惊叹，对吧？"

"梅尔·费希尔得到他发现的所有东西了吗？"丁丁问。

司机摇摇头，说："有些东西要上交给佛罗里达州，但他和他的投资人靠着剩下的宝藏发了财"。

"什么是投资人？"乔希问。

"就是借钱给梅尔·费希尔的人。"司机说，"费希尔当时不得不借很多钱来买寻宝设备，并给他的船员开工资。他变得富有之后，就把黄金作为回报送给他的投资人了!"

司机对着后视镜笑着说:"他当时要是让我投资就好了!"

几分钟后,孩子们和司机说了再见,他们跳下电车,跑回家,冲进了哈撒韦奶奶的厨房。

"孩子们,早上过得怎么样?"她问。

"我们坐了电车,奶奶!"露丝说,"司机人很好!"

"他把我们送到了梅尔·费希尔的博物馆。"丁丁说。

"我们还遇到了两个潜水寻宝的人。"乔希补充道,"我们上了他们的船,还看到了真正的金币!"

哈撒韦奶奶笑了。"太好了,你们已经见过一些宝藏啦。"她的双眼炯炯有神,"现在让我来向你们介绍一下我们的两个特殊伙伴!他们的名字是斯派克和奇普。"

第四章

"奶奶,您是怎么认识斯派克和奇普的?"露丝问。

"洗个手,来吃午餐,我来告诉你们。"哈撒韦奶奶回答。

孩子们挤在厨房的水槽前,洗好了手。

"几周前,斯派克和奇普来了我的高级会所。"哈撒韦奶奶说着,往桌上放了一盘三明治。

孩子们擦了擦手,坐了下来。

"他们把找到宝藏的事情都告诉我们了!"哈撒韦奶奶把柠檬水倒进杯子里,继续说,"现在他们在寻找投资者。"

"和梅尔·费希尔一样!"丁丁说着,伸手拿了一个金枪鱼三明治。

"没错,丁丁。"哈撒韦奶奶说。

乔希把三个三明治堆放在自己的盘子里。"您会因此发财吗?"他问。

哈撒韦奶奶笑了起来。"我们都要看情况。"她说,"不管怎样,我们每个人都在考虑投资一万美元!"

"奶奶!"露丝说。

哈撒韦奶奶的眼睛闪闪发光。"我知道,这是有点吓人。"

"伙计们,如果他们是去潜水寻宝,我愿意和他们一起去!"乔希说。

"这倒提醒了我。"奶奶说着,从操作台上拿出三件礼物,"圣诞快乐!"

"哇,谢谢奶奶!"露丝说。

"谢谢！"丁丁和乔希说。

"你们的礼物都是一样的。"哈撒韦奶奶说，"这样你们就不需要和别人分享了。"

孩子们拆开了礼物的包装。

包装纸里是一本书，叫作《在佛罗里达州寻找沉没的宝藏》。

书的封面上有一艘船，和梅尔·费希尔的船差不多，船下方有一艘沉船，潜水员正在搜寻残骸，打捞宝藏。

"我认为你们会想了解一些有关沉船的知识的。"哈撒韦奶奶说，"而且说不准我就要投资一艘了。"

"太好了！"乔希说，"谢谢您！"

哈撒韦奶奶站了起来。"不客气。我现在很忙，斯派克和奇普一小时后就会到这里来！你们能帮我布置一下客厅吗？"

"当然。"丁丁说，"您想让我们做什么？"

"我需要十把折叠椅，它们就在客厅的壁橱里。然后再搬出三张牌桌。"

孩子们在客厅里布置桌椅。哈撒韦奶奶在其

中一张桌子上放了满满一盘饼干。

"我们能留下来参加这场会议吗?"露丝问。

"当然!"奶奶说,"希望你们读了那些书之后,能问一些不错的问题!"

孩子们带着书到前廊去了。

"看。"乔希说,"书中有一整章是关于梅尔·费希尔的。"

露丝指着一张地图,地图上标着沉船的位置。"这些沉船都在佛罗里达州的近海处。"她说,"如果每艘船上都有宝藏,想一想,那得是多少钱啊!"

乔希躺在门廊上,闭上了眼睛。"你们回家的时候,我就不走了,我要成为一个宝藏猎人!"他说。

丁丁笑了。"你找宝藏?你今天早上连你的短裤都没找到,乔希!"

乔希用膝盖顶了一下丁丁。"请叫我乔希船长!"

就在这时,一辆车停了下来。两位灰头发的女士从车中出来,走向这栋房子。

A to Z 神秘案件

"我要去帮帮奶奶。"露丝说。

"我们也去。"丁丁说。他用手肘推了推乔希,说:"来吧,乔希船长!"

他们还没来得及进去,只见一辆黄色的出租车又停下了。斯派克和奇普从车上下来,斯派克手里还提着一个木质的箱子。他们都穿着干净的

裤子、熨好的衬衫和凉鞋。

"嘿!"当这两个人走上人行道时,乔希和他们打了一声招呼。

斯派克和奇普盯着孩子们,愣了片刻。最终,奇普向他们挥了挥手。"你们在这儿干什么?你们住在附近吗?"露丝笑着说:"不,我们在我奶奶家做客,这是她的家!"

斯派克笑了。"世界真小。"他说。

"我能帮你把箱子搬进去吗?"乔希问。

斯派克耸耸肩。"它很重。"

"我可以帮忙。"丁丁说。他沿着人行道跑上前去,斯派克把箱子递给了他们。

他们把沉重的箱子搬上台阶时,乔希咧嘴一笑,说:"我手指都勒疼了!"

第五章

哈撒韦奶奶的客厅挤满了人，斯派克和奇普坐在一张小桌子旁，箱子则被放在他们面前。三个孩子坐在楼梯上。

"感谢大家的光临！"哈撒韦奶奶向大家说完，朝斯派克微笑致意，斯派克随即站了起来。

"谢谢您的邀请。"斯派克说，"这几年，奇普和我一直在潜水。几周前，我们发现了一艘沉船。"

奇普打开箱子,斯派克从里面拿出一个高约8英寸[1]的金质十字架。十字架在阳光明媚的房间里闪着金光。

有人惊呼:"噢,我的天哪!"斯派克轻轻地把十字架放在桌子上。

然后他拿出一大块闪亮的银子,足足有一块肥皂那么大。然后,他又在桌子上撒了一把金币。

"海底还有更多的宝藏。"他说,"我们找到了金链子、银质高脚杯,甚至珠宝。"

奶奶的朋友们从座位上站了起来,围在斯派克和奇普周围。

"我们能摸一下吗?"一位女士问。

斯派克笑了。"不会弄坏的,女士。它在海底躺了大约400年呢!"

乔希站起身,想要看得更清楚一些。哈撒韦奶奶的朋友们正纷纷传看这些财宝。

"嗯,斯派克,"乔希说,"你是怎么把它清

---

1. 英美制长度单位。1英寸=0.0254米。——编者

理得这么干净的？它的表面不应该长满藤壶之类的东西吗？"

斯派克咧嘴笑了。"问得好！"他说，"我们先把这些物件打湿，然后用普通的陈醋擦拭。非常容易就能清洗干净。"

露丝举起手来。"我能问个问题吗？"

斯派克点了点头。"问吧。"

"梅尔·费希尔花了20年时间才找到他的沉船，"露丝说，"你们是怎么这么快就找到这艘沉船的？"

斯派克笑着说："我想我们只是幸运而已。"

"我们的地图也很精确。"奇普补充道。

斯派克转过身来面向大家。"我希望你们都能考虑投资我们。"他说，"一旦我们买到更多的设备，就可以开始打捞一些更有价值的宝藏。"

哈撒韦奶奶站了起来，说道："我们为什么不吃些点心呢？"

于是大家开始一边聊天，一边往自己的小盘子里装饼干。露丝走进厨房，去拿柠檬汁。

丁丁和乔希仍坐在楼梯上，旁边就是放满点

心的小吃桌。

斯派克和奇普走到小吃桌前。丁丁看到斯派克拿了几块饼干。

斯派克低声对他的朋友说:"这些饼干鼓鼓的,全是巧克力豆。"

丁丁正想对斯派克说些什么,但话到嘴边又被他咽了回去。他想起自己之前听过类似的话!

他闭上眼睛,仔细回忆他在机场听到的声

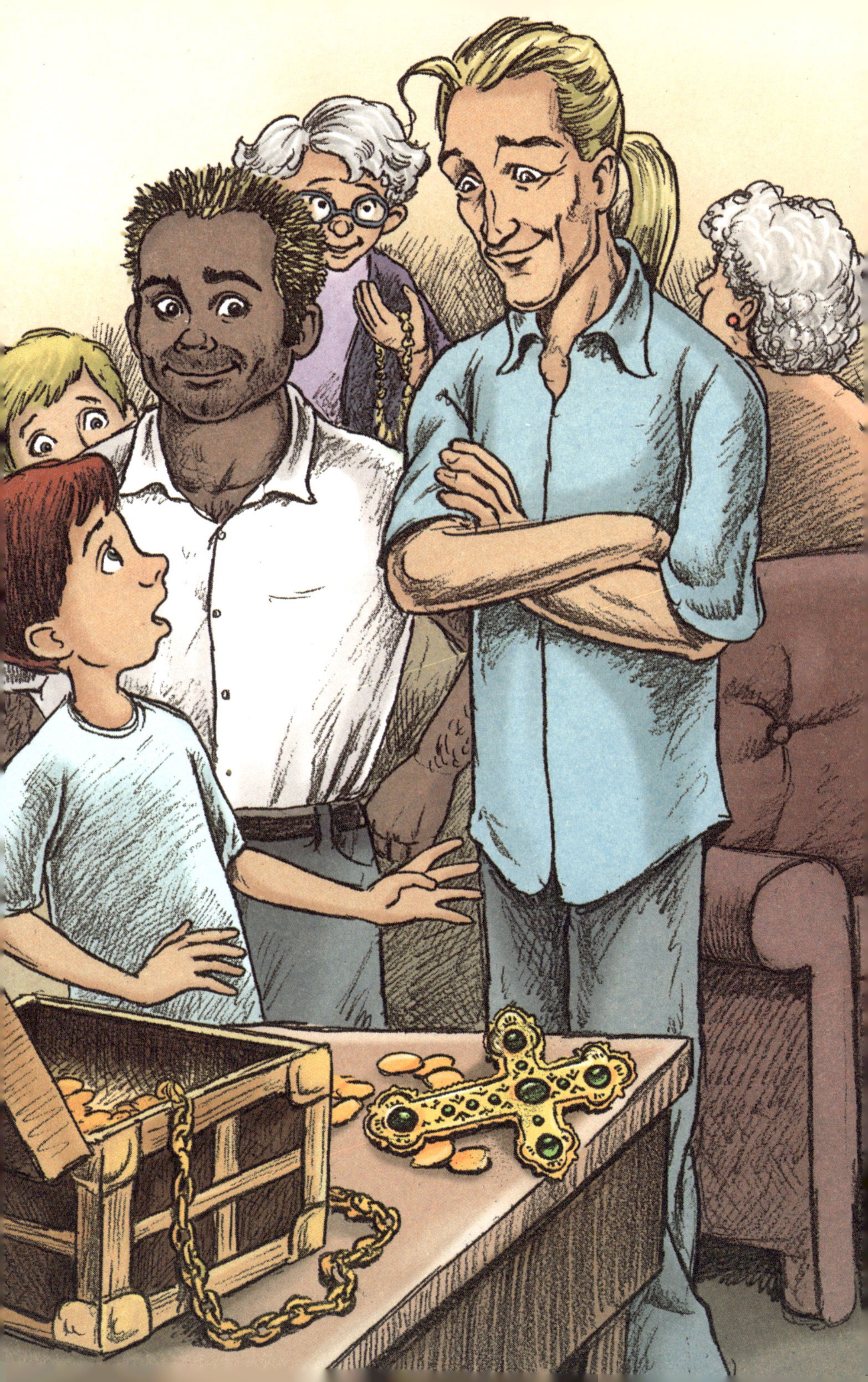

音。他非常确信当时那个人说过"这些老家伙的腰包鼓鼓的"。

丁丁差不多可以确定,这是同一个声音!

他低下头,想要寻找那个文身,但斯派克的裤子盖住了他的脚踝。

凉鞋看起来是同一款,但佛罗里达州的很多人都穿棕色皮凉鞋。

"怎么了?"露丝问丁丁,"你的脸色很难看,看起来像闻到了什么臭东西。"

丁丁站了起来。"出来一下,"他低声说,"有要紧事!"

第六章

乔希和露丝跟着丁丁穿过客厅来到门廊,坐在门前的台阶上。

"怎么了?"乔希问,"我还没吃完饼干呢!"

"还记得我昨天在机场跟你们说的那个人吗?"丁丁问,"打电话的那个!"

露丝咧嘴笑了。"记得啊,你以为有个厨师正在策划抢劫。"

丁丁转过身,透过纱门往里看了看。"我觉得那个人就是斯派克!"他说。

乔希和露丝瞪大了眼睛看着他。

乔希说:"丁丁,你在说什么?"

"我认出他的声音了!"丁丁说,"机场的那个人说了类似的话,他说'这些老家伙的腰包鼓鼓的'。"

乔希摇摇头。"所以呢?"

"你还不明白吗?"丁丁说,"也许他的意思是哈撒韦奶奶的朋友们的腰包鼓鼓的——里面都是钱!"

突然,门开了,哈撒韦奶奶的朋友们开始陆续离开。他们似乎对投资斯派克和奇普这事感到很兴奋。

然后,斯派克和奇普搬着装满金子的箱子走了出来,哈撒韦奶奶跟着他们走到了门廊处。

"谢谢您给我们叫出租车,哈撒韦太太。"斯派克说,"您真的认为您的朋友会帮助我们吗?"

哈撒韦奶奶微笑着说:"我毫不怀疑。我周一早上就和我的银行经理说这件事!"

一辆黄色的出租车靠边停了下来，斯派克和奇普带着箱子上了车。出租车开动了，他们向窗外挥手致意。

"很有意思吧？"哈撒韦奶奶说着，向房子走去。"如果有谁还没吃饱的话，这里还有很多好吃的！"她的声音透过纱门传了出来。

"谢谢奶奶！"露丝说。

"奶奶很兴奋。"哈撒韦奶奶进去之后，露丝补充道。

"如果我马上就要发财了，我也会很兴奋。"乔希说。

丁丁站了起来。"我不认为她马上就要发财了。"他说，"我觉得她马上就要被劫财了！"

"被劫财？"露丝惊呼。

"是的。"丁丁说，"斯派克和奇普会拿走奶奶的钱，然后卷款逃跑。"

"但是他们刚才给我们看的那些金子要如何解释呢？"乔希问。

丁丁摇摇头。"这个我就不清楚了，我只知道我亲耳听见的事情。"

A to Z 神秘案件

"这都是你自以为是的想法。"乔希说,"再说了,你不能确定那就是斯派克,打电话的那个人你都没见过。"

"但我看见他的脚了!"丁丁说完,把那个人脚踝有文身的事告诉了乔希和露丝。

"还好我十分敏锐。"乔希说,"我知道我们该怎么解决这件事了。"

"怎么解决?"露丝问。

"确定丁丁听到的那个打电话的人到底是不是斯派克。"

丁丁看着他。"那我们该怎么做呢,这位敏锐的朋友?"

乔希咧嘴笑了。"放轻松,让斯派克给我们看他的文身就行啦!"

第七章

"好主意!"丁丁说,"我们去码头吧。"

"等一下!"露丝说着,打开纱门,拿了几条毛巾,喊道,"奶奶,我们要去海滩了!"

走在路上时,露丝把毛巾扔给两位伙伴。"如果斯派克还穿着长裤呢?"她问。

"丁丁会想出办法的。"乔希说着,对丁丁咧嘴一笑,"对吧?"

丁丁摇摇头。"这可是你的主意。况且,敏锐的人可是你啊!"

他们一边走一边想对策。当他们到达码头时,仍然没有想出办法。

"我知道了!"乔希说,"我跟他说,丁丁正在考虑弄个文身!让斯派克把他的文身给我们看看!"

丁丁笑了,说:"小孩是不能有文身的,乔希。"

不一会儿,孩子们到了斯派克和奇普停船的地方。但船不在那里。

"他们走了!"露丝说。

"现在怎么办?"丁丁问,"要等他们回来吗?"

"不如我们在海滩上逛一逛?"乔希提议,"那样的话,我们就可以一边玩,一边留意船什么时候回来了。"

"好吧。"露丝说,"但是我们不能在外面待到太晚,奶奶会担心的。"

"最后跑到的是小狗!"乔希喊着,迅速从码头跳到了海滩上。

孩子们下海游泳,在海滩上捡贝壳,丁丁和

露丝还把乔希埋到了沙子里。到了5点，他们的皮肤因晒伤和海盐的刺激而发痒。

"看，那是不是他们的船？"露丝问。

一艘白色的船停在码头的尽头。

"我觉得是！"乔希说，"走！"

孩子们沿着码头跑了过去，跑到船边时，看到奇普正在固定绳索。斯派克站在方向盘后面，准备关闭发动机。

两人都穿着T恤衫和牛仔裤。斯派克的脚脖子还是被盖住了。

"你们去潜水了吗？"乔希问。

"我们每天都潜水。"斯派克回答。他走上码头，拍了拍他的肚子。"我要去吃几个汉堡。能走了吗，奇普？"他说。

孩子们跟着斯派克和奇普走到码头的尽头，然后互相道别。

在回奶奶家的路上，露丝说："我们还是没有看到文身。"

"确实，但我看到了别的东西。"丁丁说，"他们涂好了那艘船的名字，叫'金鹅号'。"

金鹅号

乔希看着他,问:"所以呢?"

"机场的那个人说了一些关于把鹅淹死的话。"丁丁说,"也许他谈论的'鹅'就是这艘船!"

"但这是什么意思呢?"露丝问,"船可不会被淹死。"

丁丁摇了摇头,说:"这我就不知道了"

几分钟后,他们看到了哈撒韦奶奶,她正在花园里除杂草。

"嘿,奶奶!"露丝和她打招呼。

奶奶抬起头挥手致意。

"明天我们再去找他们一次。"丁丁压低声音说,"你们和我一起吗?"

"如果斯派克还穿着长裤呢?"露丝问。

"那我就实施我的计划。"丁丁说。

"什么计划?"乔希问。

"跟他说我们要举办文身比赛。"丁丁说。

乔希盯着丁丁,说:"什么比赛?"

"我刚想到的。"丁丁边说边轻拍乔希的头,"我要在码头旁边贴一张关于文身比赛的海报,再把比赛的事告诉斯派克和奇普。如果斯派克的脚踝上有文身,他也许自己就会提起,甚至还会向我们展示他的文身。"

"丁丁又在做白日梦了。"乔希压低了声音对露丝说。

"我觉得这很棒!"露丝说,"干吧,我向奶奶要些纸和笔!"

第八章

丁丁从床上跳起来,摇了摇乔希的肩膀。"乔希,起来!我们要去码头了!"他说。

乔希睁开一只眼睛。"几点了?"他还没有睡醒,迷迷糊糊地问。

丁丁瞥了一眼他旁边的钟。"快8点了,快点!"

丁丁穿上短裤和T恤衫。洗漱完,他梳好头

58

发，拿上了昨晚画的那张海报。

"快点，乔希！"他一边说着，一边匆匆下了楼。

露丝坐在桌边，正往面包圈上抹花生酱。

"奶奶上午去游泳了。"她说着，将一盘面包圈推到丁丁面前，"乔希呢？"

丁丁坐下来，伸手去拿草莓酱。"刚起床呢。"他说。

丁丁打开海报时，乔希跌跌撞撞地走进厨房，他的红头发直直地立了起来。"希望这个计划能成功。"他说，"我梦见我变成了弥达斯国王，我碰过的东西都会变成巧克力！"

乔希拿起一个面包圈，睡眼惺忪地看了看丁丁的海报。在海报的底部，丁丁画了一个有着猫头鹰文身的手臂。

A to Z 神秘案件

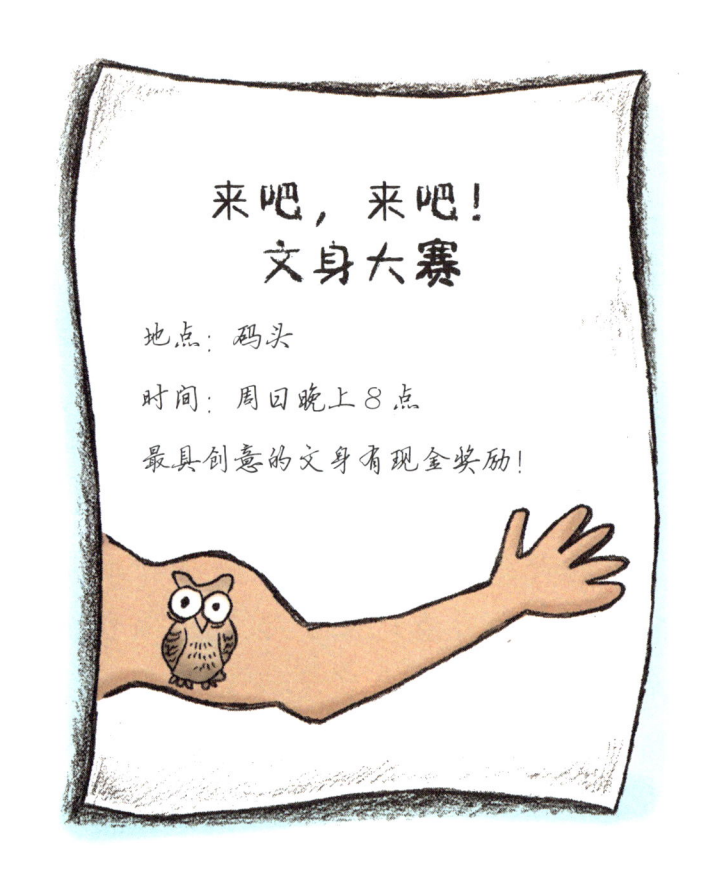

> ## 来吧，来吧！
> ## 文身大赛
>
> 地点：码头
>
> 时间：周日晚上8点
>
> 最具创意的文身有现金奖励！

"万一到时候一群有文身的人来到现场，却发现没有比赛，怎么办？"乔希问。

丁丁耸耸肩。"反正我们必须得确认斯派克脚踝上是否有文身。你能想出别的办法吗？"

乔希耸了耸肩。

"好吧，既然如此，我们走吧。"丁丁说。

他们每人拿了一个苹果,朝码头走去。丁丁拿上了海报和四枚图钉。

尽管现在时间还很早,但码头上已经有不少人了。丁丁把海报钉在一根灯柱上。

"好了,我们现在去找斯派克和奇普吧。"他说。随即他们匆匆往码头赶去。

有些人在他们自己的船上喝着咖啡,享受着清晨的阳光。那艘名为"金鹅号"的船被缆绳固定在码头上。

船上一点声音也没有。

"他们是不是还在睡觉?"乔希问。

丁丁耸耸肩。"我没有听到打鼾的声音。"

露丝透过一个圆形的舷窗向里面望去。"里面没人。"她说。

"看,门是开着的。"乔希说,"他们一定在里面。"

丁丁走上甲板,敲了敲木门。"嘿!"他问,"有人在吗?"

然后他跳回码头上。"也许他们出去吃早餐了。"他说,"我们等等吧。"

A to Z 神秘案件

孩子们坐在阳光下。一只鹈鹕在码头上一摇一摆地走着,在每艘船前都停留了一会儿。一位女士给它扔了些面包。

乔希拿出他的书,读了起来。

"看这个。"他说,"金子不管在海底放了多久,都会闪闪发光。但银子需要在一种特殊的化学溶液中浸泡几天,才能恢复光泽。"

乔希抬起头来。"昨天,斯派克跟大家说,他们清洗金子和银子用的是陈醋!"

孩子们你看着我,我看着你。

丁丁站起来,踏上了"金鹅号"。他在甲板上走来走去,仔细观察了每一个角落。

他看见一个氧气罐斜靠在长凳旁,便停下来去察看一番,然后回了码头。

"那个氧气罐是空的。"他对乔希和露丝说。

"你怎么知道的?"乔希问。

"上面有个圆形仪表盘,"丁丁说,"小箭头指着字母E。"

"也许是他们用光了所有氧气,还没有给它充气。"

"有可能。"丁丁说,"但我没有看到任何其他潜水设备。"

露丝走近甲板。"也许他们把设备放在了船里。"她看了看伙伴们,"我认为我们应该去检查一下。"

"我也这么认为。"丁丁说。

乔希回头,朝码头看了看。"如果我们偷看的时候,他们回来了,把我们逮个正着,怎么办?"他说。

"我们可以说是奶奶派我们来的。"露丝说,"我可以说奶奶还有问题想问他们。"

"我觉得他们抓住海盗的话,会把海盗吊死。"乔希说。

"乔希,只是看看别人的船而已,这并不代表我们就是海盗。"露丝说,"如果他们想骗我奶奶,我会查出来的!走,我们不会碰任何东西,我们只是看看。"

她跳上船,从楼梯进入船舱。乔希和丁丁紧随其后。

三个人挤在小小的船舱中间。"好臭!"露

丝说。

"房间里很乱,是吧?"乔希说。床铺没有整理过,小厨房里乱七八糟地堆着脏盘子和玻璃杯。饭桌上粘满了黏稠的污渍。

丁丁往几个黑暗的角落瞥了几眼:"我还是没有看见——"

"嘘!有声音!"露丝说着,往上指了指。一时间,他们都听见了脚步声。

孩子们瞪大了眼睛看着彼此。

乔希的脸色变得煞白。

金鹅号的宝藏

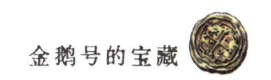

丁丁环顾小船舱,朝后方的一扇窄门冲了过去。

他推开门,示意乔希和露丝跟上。

第九章

孩子们挤在船上的小浴室里。

这个地方没空间让孩子们坐下或转身,于是孩子们只能挤着站在一起,你看看我,我看看你。

突然,楼梯上方传来沉重的脚步声。他们屏住了呼吸。

他们先是听到砰的一声,随后是更重的一声。然后又传来一阵脚步声,这一次是上楼梯的声音。

这个小房间十分闷热,汗水流进丁丁的眼睛,他快不能呼吸了。

他们又等了一会儿,但这次没有听见别的声音。

"我闻到了炒鸡蛋的味道!"乔希在丁丁的耳边轻声说。

丁丁翻了个白眼。

"我真的闻到了!"乔希说。

几分钟后,丁丁把门打开了一条缝,凉爽的空气涌进浴室。

他迅速环顾四周,听到上面有人说话的声音,又把门轻轻地关上了。

"他们在甲板上。"他说,"我们不能继续待在这间浴室里。如果他们有人想用浴室,我们就完了!"

"我们为什么不一走了之呢?"乔希问。

"那要怎么解释我们躲在他们的船上这件事?"露丝说,"现在走已经来不及了!"

丁丁溜出浴室,发现地板上有一扇活板门。

他跪下来,把活板门拉开。乔希和露丝则踮着脚走出了浴室。

突然,孩子们听到发动机的轰鸣声,丁丁感觉到船动了起来——船正在向后移动!

"他们要开船了!"他低声说,"来,快下来!"

孩子们仓皇失措地跑到下层的船舱里。丁丁关上了头顶的门。他们身处黑暗中,只有活板门周围有一丝光亮。

"这个地方臭得要死!"乔希说。

"现在怎么办?"露丝问。

"不知道。"丁丁回答道。

想了一会儿,他接着说:"他们肯定是要去潜水点。我们得躲起来,直到他们返回码头。"

"但他们可能要去一整天!"乔希说。

孩子们来回扭动着身子,想尽量让自己舒服一点。

丁丁顺着活板门的门缝往上看,他看到了桌子的底部。桌子右边是通向甲板的楼梯。

"噢!"乔希突然说,"我想我坐在船锚上了!"

"煤渣蹭伤了我的膝盖!"露丝说。

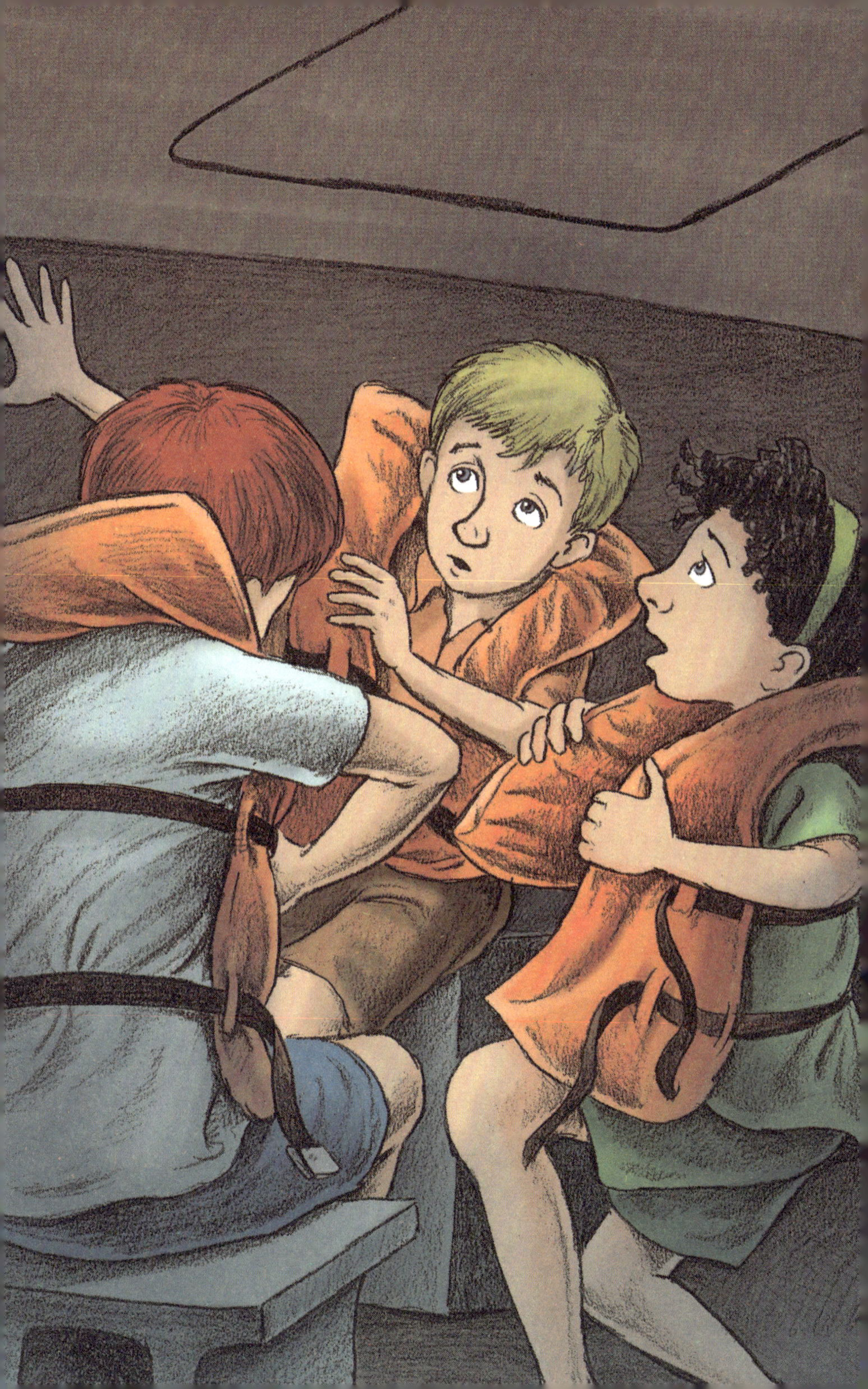

丁丁用手在那块倾斜的木地板上摸索着,他感受到地板表面的坚硬、粗糙,这里有很多煤渣。

然后他摸到了一些湿软的东西。

"伙计们,我找到了一些救生衣。"丁丁低声说,"穿上吧!"

孩子们艰难地穿上了救生衣。丁丁一直盯着门缝看,他想知道斯派克或奇普是否进入了船舱。

"上这艘船是谁的馊主意?"乔希说,"我觉得自己像个囚犯!"

"你之前说想去潜水。"丁丁说,"你的愿望终于实现了!"

"是啊。"乔希说,"但我没说要被关在这个臭气熏天的地牢里!"

丁丁通过门缝看到了一个人影闪过。有人正打着赤脚下楼梯!

"嘘!"他说,"他们过来了!"

他们听到了脚步声,然后是人说话的声音。人影在活板门上来回移动。

"这地方跟猪圈一样。"其中一人说。丁丁认出那是斯派克的声音。

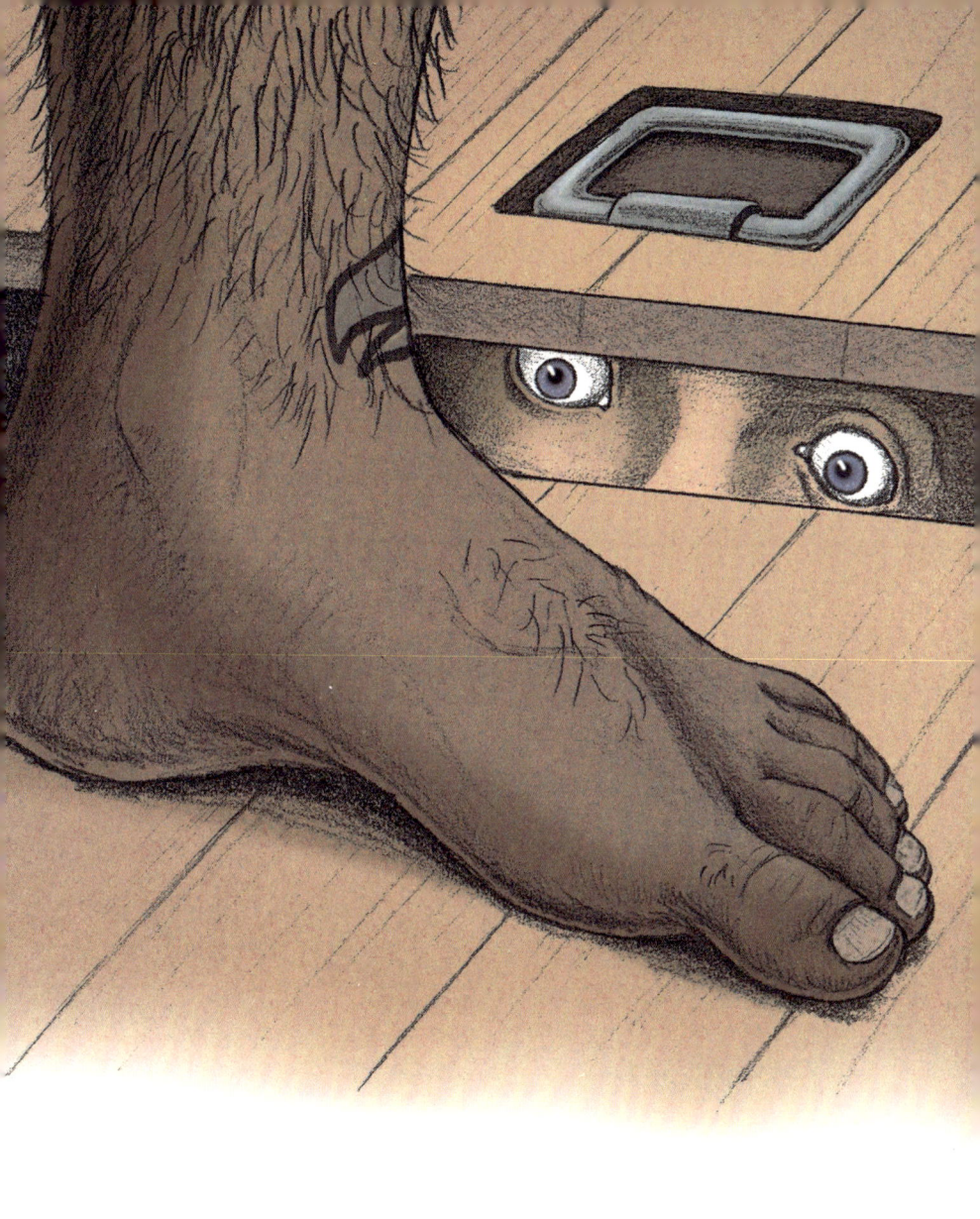

"干吗费劲打扫呢?"奇普咯咯地笑着回应,"很快,它就真干净了。"

丁丁听到了什么东西移动的声音,然后他的

头顶传来砰的一声。

透过门缝,他看到了细细的桌腿。一条凳子或一把椅子被拖到了那张小桌子旁边。

"有果汁吗?"斯派克问。

"不一定。"奇普回答,"不过我想应该有牛奶。"

"他们在吃早餐!"乔希在丁丁的耳边轻声说,"我就说我闻到了炒鸡蛋的味道!"

随后有人在桌子旁坐了下来。丁丁可以看到那个人的小腿。

那条腿黝黑且长满腿毛。

突然,丁丁吸了口凉气,离他眼睛几英寸的地方,他看到了一个文身。

那是一个鹰头。

第十章

斯派克就是他在机场中无意听到在蓄谋抢劫的那个人!

这时,奇普说话了。"嘿,"他说,"这个旧浴缸没了,我会想念它的。"

"我可不会。"斯派克回应,"只要我们从那些老家伙那里拿到钱,我就去买一辆佛罗里达州最炫酷的车。我受够了像沙丁鱼一样过着这样贫穷的生活！"

"那你想什么时候动手？"奇普问。

"等我吃完饭。"斯派克说，"我甚至会让你享受一下玩斧头的快感。"

丁丁听到奇普笑了起来。"我们装了这么多煤渣，这艘船在10秒钟内就会沉没！"他说。

"是的。"斯派克说，"别忘了那个箱子，那个可不能沉了！"

乔希捏了捏丁丁的手臂。另一边，露丝轻轻地吸了一口气。

斯派克和奇普要让"金鹅号"沉没！

"别担心。"奇普说，"我已经把金子放进小皮艇里了。"

椅子移动的声音响了起来，随后带有文身的脚踝从丁丁的视线中消失了。

"等这只鹅沉没了，我们就开着小皮艇回城里去。"斯派克说，"我们低调行事，从那些老家伙那里拿到他们的钱。"

他笑了笑。"然后我们就人间蒸发。"

金鹅号的宝藏

丁丁心一沉,随即又听到了砰砰声和脚步声。

斯派克说:"确认一下,不要把标着你名字的东西留在船上。你知道的,纸会浮在水面上。"

"别担心。"奇普说,"斧头在哪儿?"

谈话声渐渐变得模糊。

"你们听到了吗?"乔希问,"他们要把这艘

船弄沉!"

"嘘!"丁丁发出嘘声。突然,孩子们听到一声接一声的撞击声。

丁丁倒吸一口凉气。这是在用斧头劈木质的船身!

然后,他听到砰的一声,接着是有人从船舱的楼梯向上跑的脚步声。

突然,一个新的声音传来,是潺潺的水流声,海水正涌进船里!

"就是现在!"丁丁说着,推开了活板门迅速爬了出去。乔希和露丝跟在他身后。

他们脚下都是海水。

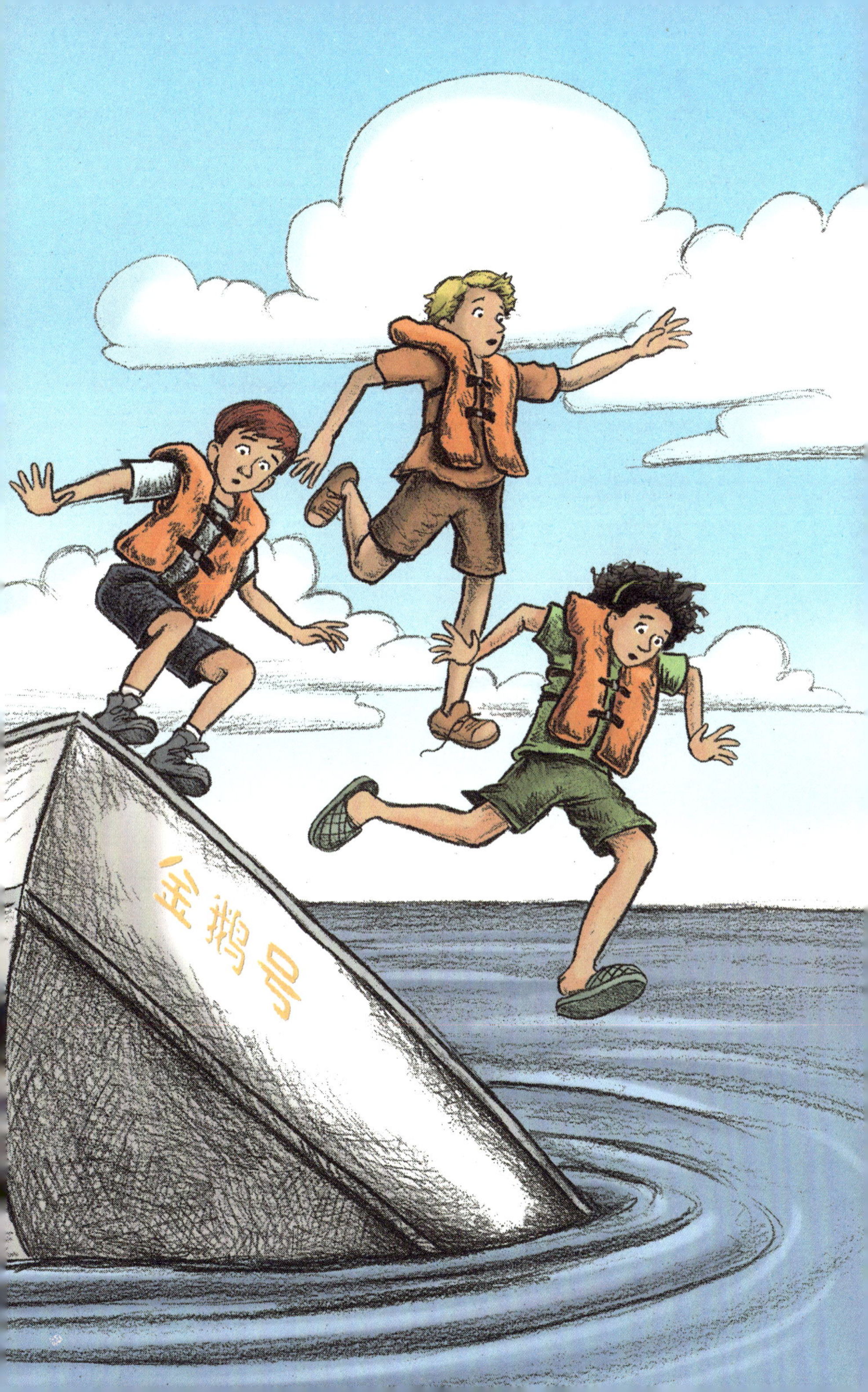
金鹅号

"看!"露丝指着船舱一侧的一个洞。海水正从那里灌进来。

"我们该怎么办?"乔希问。

丁丁爬上楼梯偷偷看了看。他看见斯派克和奇普驾驶着小皮艇离开了。

"他们走了!"丁丁说,"快来!"

孩子们跑上楼梯,冲向船尾。

乔希低头,看着下面的海水。"我们现在该怎么办?"他尖声叫道。

"往海里跳!"露丝喊道。

随后他们就跳进了海里。

第十一章

丁丁感觉水淹到了他的头顶，他来不及闭上嘴，海水就灌进了他的嘴里。咸咸的海水还刺痛了他的双眼。

救生衣帮助他浮到了海面上。他漂了起来。穿着橙色救生衣的乔希和露丝漂在他的身边。

"你们还好吗？"丁丁问。

"看！"乔希指着丁丁身后说。

丁丁在水中转了个身。

"金鹅号"歪向一边,几秒钟后,便沉入了大海。

当船沉入水中时,孩子们听到哗的一声巨响!

"还好我们及时跳下了船!"乔希说。

"我们游起来吧!"丁丁说,"斯派克和奇普可能会回来确认船是不是沉没了!"

"往哪儿游?"乔希问,"我甚至看不到陆地!"

"但我看到别的船了。"露丝用湿淋淋的胳膊指了指,"看到那些伸出水面的东西了吗?"

乔希用手划起水来。"我觉得那是鲨鱼的鱼鳍!"他叫了起来。

露丝笑了。"鲨鱼可没有白色的帆,乔希。"

孩子们开始朝那些船游去。突然,丁丁听到一声轰鸣。

他转头,以为斯派克和奇普追上来了。但是,他看到了一艘白色的大船,船身上,黑色字体赫然写着"海岸警卫队"。

船飞驰而来,然后慢了下来。孩子们在波涛中摇摆起伏。

"你们在干什么?"一个声音从船上传来。

丁丁看见一个穿着白色制服的人站在甲板上。他拿着扩音器,怒视着他们。

丁丁想叫喊几声,但一波巨浪往他的嘴里灌满了海水。

另一个人把三个救生圈扔进水里。"抓住那些救生圈!"那个穿白制服的人大叫着。

三个救生圈被抛在了离他们不远的地方。

不一会儿,丁丁、乔希和露丝就被拖到了甲板上。

孩子们依偎在一起。一群人站在周围盯着他们。

太阳很温暖,但是丁丁还是止不住地发抖。

其中一个人给他们披上毯子。

"怎么样啦?"穿制服的人说,"我等着你们开口呢。"

他用奇怪的表情盯着孩子们,说:"但愿你们会说英语。"

乔希咧嘴笑了。"我们会说,你们有什么吃的吗?我快饿死了!"

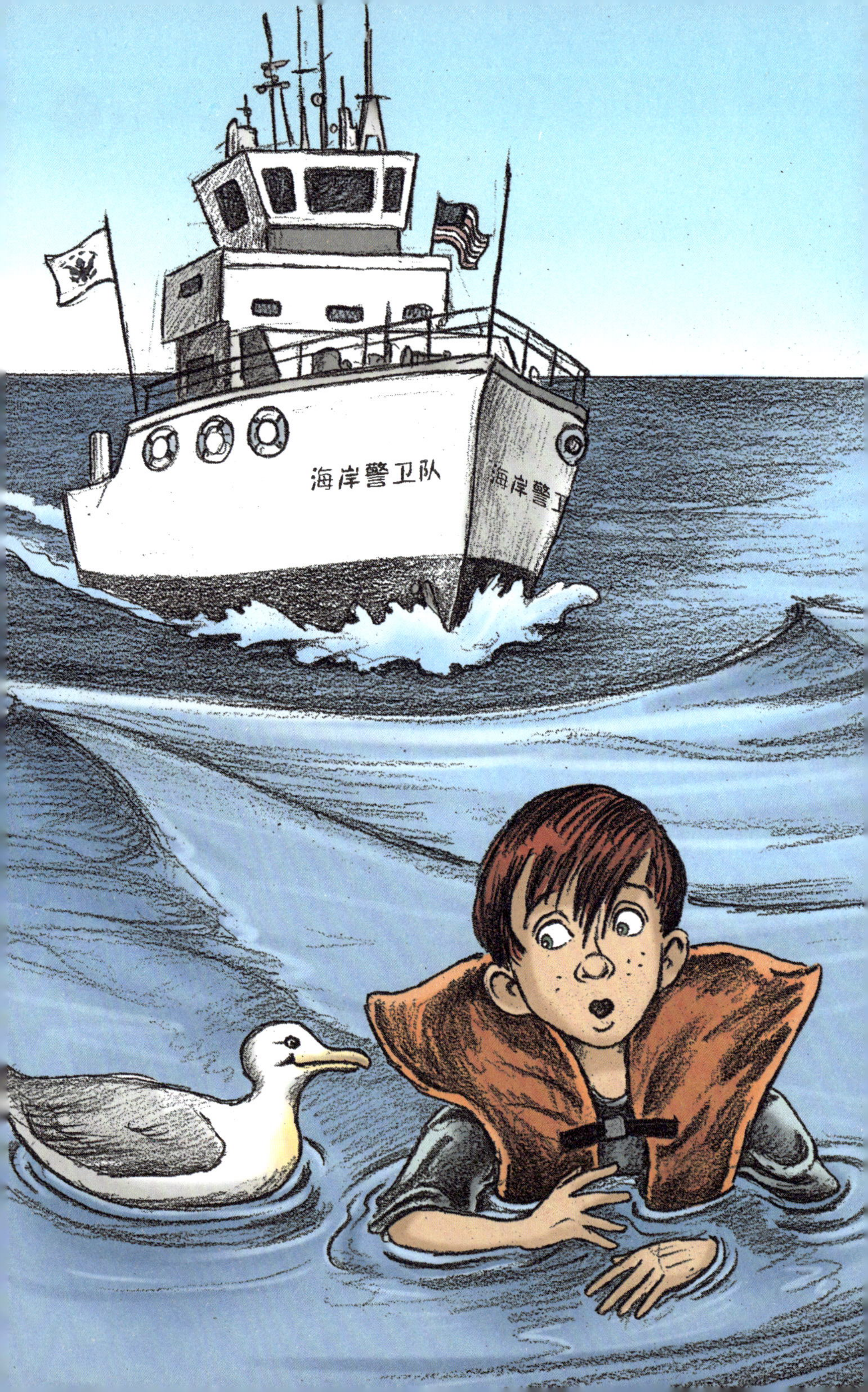
海岸警卫队
海岸警卫

金鹅号的宝藏

人们笑了起来。

拿着扩音器的人咧嘴一笑。"好吧,孩子们,先告诉我们,你们为什么要往古巴游。"他说,"然后我就给你们吃的!"

烟花接二连三地在天空中绽放。"太棒了!"乔希说。现在是新年前夜的10点,距他们被海

岸警卫队的船救起已经过去两天了。

孩子们躺在哈撒韦奶奶家后院的草坪上。他们刚吃了一顿龙虾大餐,每个人都饱饱的。

哈撒韦奶奶拿着一个托盘走了过来。"谁还吃得下巧克力冰激凌?"她问。

丁丁呻吟着:"再吃一口,我的肚子就要撑破了!"

乔希坐了起来。"我要吃一点!"他说。

奶奶把盘子放在毯子上。"你们随便吃。"她说完,和孩子们坐在了一起。

"今天的晚餐很丰盛,奶奶。"露丝说。

"我的荣幸!"奶奶说,"孩子们,你们都是英雄!多亏了你们,警察才抓到了斯派克和奇普。我们差点损失很多钱!"

"好吧,丁丁,"乔希说,"你是对的。在机场打电话的确实是斯派克,他的确说了'拿上票子'。"

哈撒韦奶奶握着丁丁的手。"你帮助了我们!"她说。

丁丁羞红了脸。"嗯,伙伴们也帮了很多

忙。"他说,"如果没有露丝,那两个人回来的时候,我们就不会正好在船上。他们把船弄沉后,就会带着钱逃走了。"

"是乔希发现了他们在清洗金银的事上说了谎。"露丝说,"我在书上都没注意到这个知识。"

哈撒韦奶奶笑了。"你们三个会获得一份奖励。"

"奖励?"乔希说,"为什么?"

"斯派克和奇普展示给我们看的金银是从迈阿密的一座博物馆里偷来的。"哈撒韦奶奶说,"博物馆会给你们三个一份奖励!"

"太好了——给多少钱?"乔希问。

露丝笑着说:"别贪心,乔希。"

乔希吃完最后一口冰激凌,说:"我不是贪心,我只是喜欢钱!"

突然,一个巨大的蘑菇形烟花在他们头顶绽放,红色、蓝色和绿色的火光倾泻下来。

"大家许个愿吧!"哈撒韦奶奶说。

"我希望我能吃更多冰激凌。"乔希说。

"我希望我有一台自己的电脑。"露丝说。

"我希望我们能在这里多待一会儿。"丁丁说,"我们的假期过得太快啦!"

哈撒韦奶奶吻了丁丁的脸颊。"你的愿望实现了。"她说,"这个夏天,我会邀请你们再次来这里度假!"

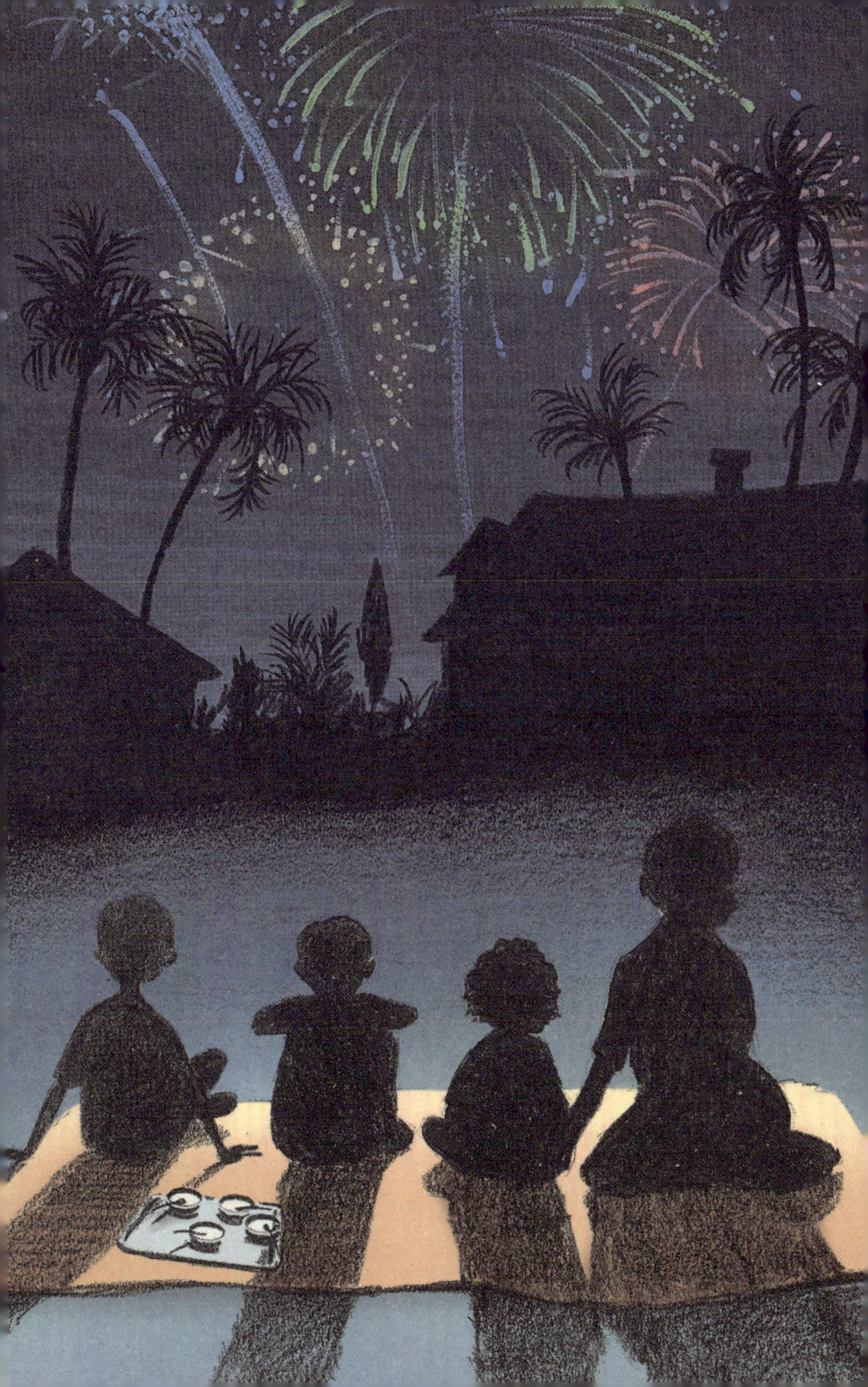

A to Z Mysteries®

The Goose's Gold

by **Ron Roy**

illustrated by
John Steven Gurney

Welcome to A to Z Mysteries on Location at Key West

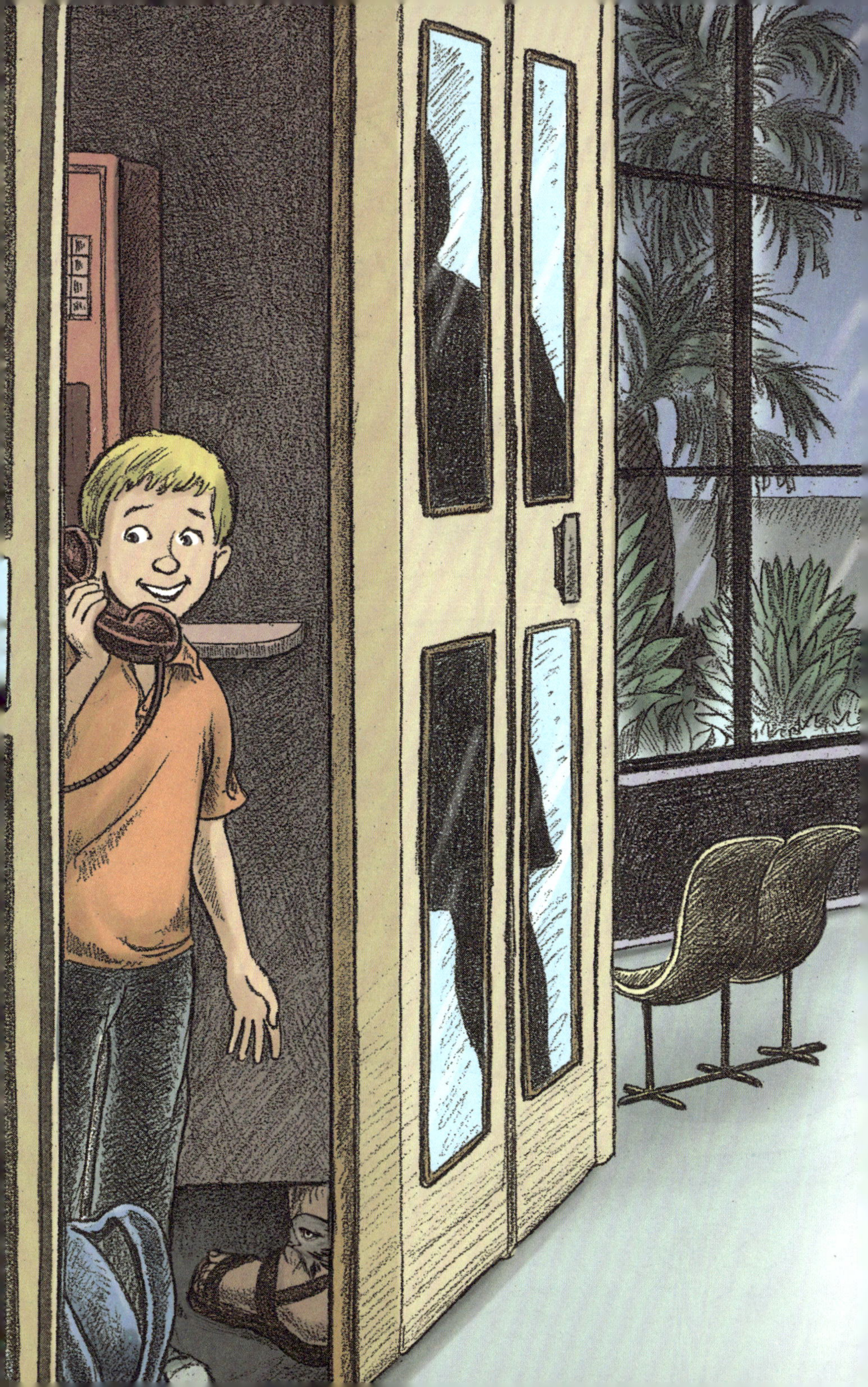

Chapter 1

"Hi, Mom, I'm in Florida!" Dink said into the phone. He glanced out the airport's large windows. "I can see palm trees! And it's about 80 degrees!"

Donald David Duncan, known as Dink to his friends, was on winter vacation from school. He, Josh, and Ruth Rose were visiting Ruth Rose's grandmother. She lived on an island called Key West.

Dink's mother told him to have a wonderful time. "And remember your manners!"

Dink grinned into the phone. "What manners? Just joking, Mom! See you in a few days."

Dink hung up the phone. As he bent over to pick up his backpack, he saw a pair of feet in the next booth. They were tan and in sandals. One hairy ankle had a tattoo of an eagle's head.

Dink heard the man's voice. He was whispering, "…then we take the dough and split. They'll never find us!"

Take the dough and split? Was this guy planning a robbery? Dink wondered.

He leaned toward the other booth so he could hear better.

"Those old cookies are loaded," the man whispered. "We get in and out, then we drown the goose and disappear!"

Dink blinked. Loaded cookies? Drown the goose? What was going on here?

Suddenly, Josh snapped his fingers in front of Dink's face. "Earth to Dink," he said.

"Come on, we have to go find my grandmother," said Ruth Rose.

Dink stepped away from the phone. He peeked into the next booth, but it was empty.

Dink hurried after Josh and Ruth Rose.

"You guys aren't gonna believe what I just heard!" he said. "I think some guy is planning a robbery!"

Josh and Ruth Rose looked at Dink. "Are you kidding?" Ruth Rose asked.

"No, honest!" Dink said.

Dink tried to imitate the way the man had whispered. "He said, 'take the dough and drown the goose!'"

Josh looked at his friend. "That's it?"

Dink nodded. "Well, he also said something about loaded cookies."

"Maybe he said 'bake the dough and brown the goose', " Ruth Rose said. "Sounds like he was a chef, not a robber."

Suddenly, they heard someone call, "Yoo-hoo, kids. Over here!"

"There she is," Ruth Rose said excitedly. "HI,

A to Z 神秘案件

GRAM!"

The kids hurried over to a smiling woman with white hair.

"Honey, how you've grown!" Ruth Rose's grandmother said. She gave Ruth Rose a hug. "Merry Christmas!"

Ruth Rose blushed. "Thanks, Gram. These are my best friends, Dink and Josh. Guys, this is Gram Hathaway!"

Gram Hathaway was short and tanned. She wore shorts, a purple T-shirt, and a baseball cap—backward!

Gram shook hands with the boys. "I've heard a lot about you two," she said. "Got your bags? Let's go home and have a nice supper."

Ruth Rose's grandmother led them through the exit doors. The evening was hot and humid. Everyone wore shorts and sandals.

"Boy, back home we had a foot of snow!" Josh said. "I can't wait to see the ocean!"

"There's a lovely beach not far from my house," Ruth Rose's gram said. "I think you'll find the water pretty warm for December."

They piled into her small white car. "Buckle up, everyone," she said.

Dink and Josh climbed in the back. Dink almost sat on a pair of in-line skates. "Just dump those on the floor," Gram said.

Josh snuck Dink a look. "Do you skate?" he asked Ruth Rose's grandmother.

She winked at Josh in the rearview mirror. "Only on Tuesdays and Fridays. The rest of the week I jog or swim!"

A few minutes later, they were zooming along a busy street. Dink watched the tall palm trees as the car whizzed past them. Through rows of neat houses, he caught glimpses of blue sea and nearly white sand.

"Look, a pelican!" Josh cried, pointing out the window.

"You'll see plenty of those here," Gram Hathaway said. "And they aren't afraid of people. I saw one swoop down and snatch a girl's ice cream cone!"

"They'd better not try that with me!" Josh said.

"Here we are," Gram Hathaway said. She pulled

A to Z 神秘案件

her car into a driveway surrounded by rosebushes.

Dink saw a small pink house with blue shutters. Window boxes were filled with bright flowers. Pots of pink geraniums sat on the front steps.

"You've got an awesome house, Mrs. Hathaway!"

Josh said.

　She laughed. "Please call me Gram, and thank you!"

　The kids followed Gram into a yellow living room. In one corner, a Christmas tree stood on a table.

"Okay, drop your bags and let's eat!"

Gram led Ruth Rose and Josh into her kitchen. "I hope you like fried chicken!"

Dink followed slowly. He couldn't stop thinking about the man on the telephone.

If he was just talking about food, Dink wondered, why was he whispering?

Chapter 2

"I smell cookies," Josh said the next morning.

Dink rolled over and looked at Josh. He was sitting up in bed with his nose in the air.

Dink grinned. "You look like a rabbit, Josh."

"No, I'm serious," Josh said. He walked over to the window and took a deep whiff. "Yep, it's cookies. With chocolate chips!"

They heard a knock on their bedroom door.

"Hurry up, you guys!" Ruth Rose said. "Gram is making breakfast!"

Dink and Josh scrambled into shorts and T-shirts. They did a quick job of washing up, then hurried down the stairs.

Gram Hathaway stood at the stove, spooning pancake batter onto a hot griddle. She was wearing running gear, and her hair was tied in a red bandanna. "Good morning, boys. How'd you sleep?"

"Great," Dink said. "Except Josh snored all night!"

"Ha!" Ruth Rose laughed as she poured orange juice into four glasses. She liked to dress all in one color. Today she was wearing green shorts, a green T-shirt, and green jelly shoes.

Josh glanced at the stove. "I thought I smelled chocolate chip cookies."

Gram smiled. "What an observant young man! There's a batch in the oven that's almost done."

Josh nudged Dink. "See? I'm an observant young man!"

Gram brought a platter of pancakes to the table. "I'm baking cookies for our company."

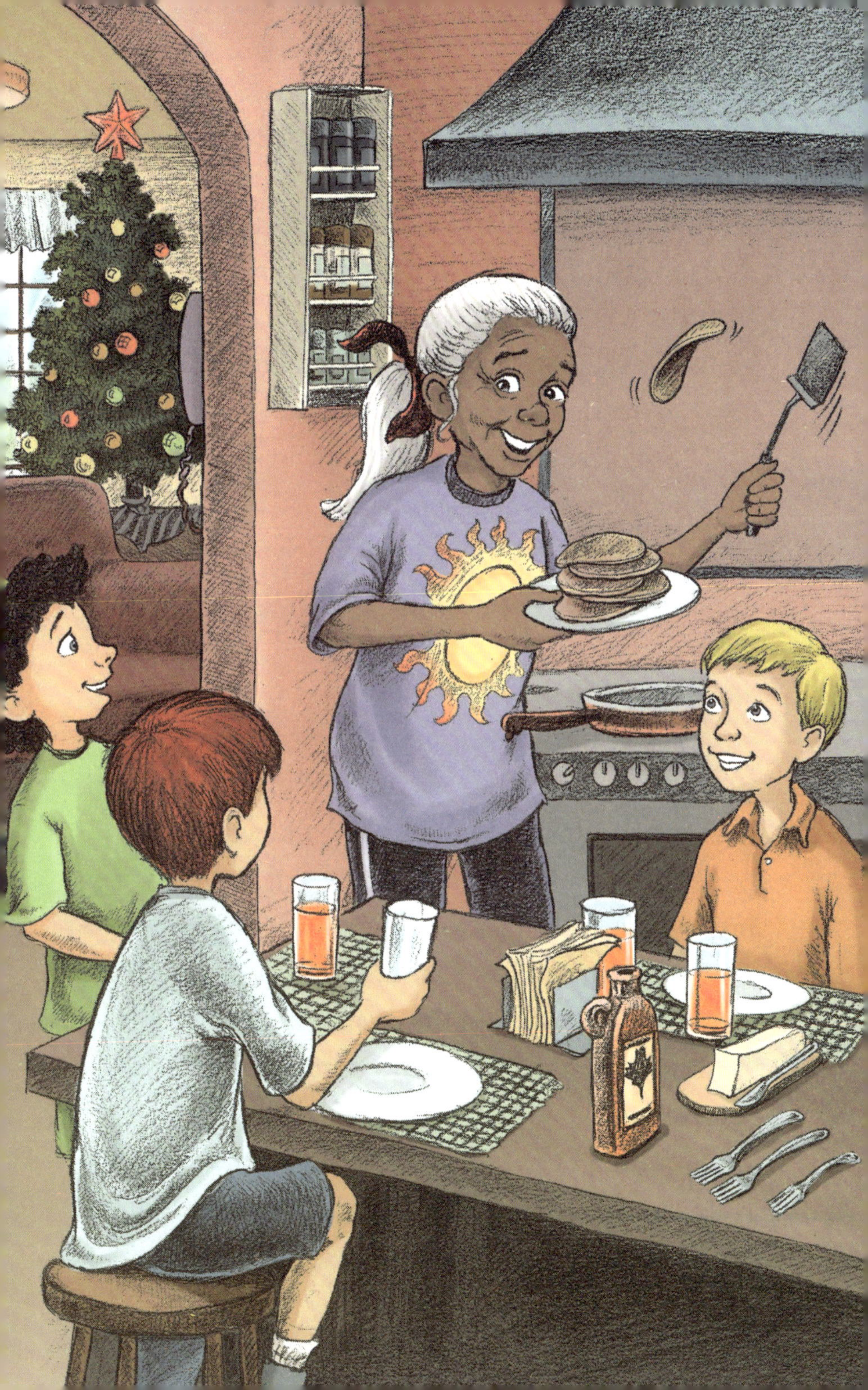

"Who's the company, Gram?" Ruth Rose asked.

Her grandmother smiled mysteriously. "It's a surprise. You'll have to wait and see."

While they ate breakfast, Gram told the kids about some of the sights to see on the island.

"Be sure to take a ride on the Old Town Trolley," she said. "It scoots all over town."

"How do we get to the beach?" Josh asked.

"Just walk to the end of my street, then turn right," Gram said. "Two more blocks, and you'll see the water!"

"Can we help you clean up?" Ruth Rose asked.

"I'll clean up after my run," Gram replied. "You kids go have fun, and I'll see you for lunch."

The kids each grabbed a warm cookie, then hurried outside.

Ten minutes later, they were carrying their sneakers and wading in the ocean.

Dink was looking at guys' feet on the beach. He saw plenty of ankle tattoos, but none were eagles.

From the beach, they walked up some steps to a wide concrete pier. There were benches and tables, and vendors selling food and souvenirs. A man was juggling oranges and grapefruits. Big gray pelicans sat on posts, waiting for tourists to feed them.

"Let's go see those boats," Josh suggested, pointing toward a long wooden dock.

The kids ran along the beach and crossed over to the dock. Dink saw a sign that said WATCH FOR SPLINTERS AND FISHHOOKS! NO BARE FEET!

People were lined up, fishing. One little girl shouted, then pulled up a silver fish the size of Dink's hand.

The kids pulled on their shoes and hiked along the long dock. Boats were nestled in slips on both sides.

Everywhere they looked, people were washing, polishing, or painting their boats.

"I wish I had a sailboat," Josh said as they continued along the dock. "I'd live on it and sail around the world."

"What about me and Dink?" Ruth Rose asked.

"Oh, I'd hire you as my cook," Josh told Ruth Rose. "You could make me cookies and pizza."

He nudged Dink with his hip. "And Dinkus could wash my clothes and make my bed!"

"Yeah, right," Dink said. "And make you walk the plank!"

"Listen! I hear music," Josh said.

A radio stood at the end of the dock next to a man holding a paintbrush. He was painting curly gold letters on the side of a white boat. So far, he'd finished G and O.

Smears of gold speckled the man's tanned fingers. He was short, but the muscles on his arms made him look like a weightlifter.

Another man stood next to him, eating a muffin. He was tall and skinny, with a blond ponytail. Both men wore tank tops over baggy jeans.

The skinny man nodded at the kids. "Howdy," he said.

"I like your boat," said Josh. "Do you live on it?"

The skinny man turned down the radio. "There're two beds up front," he said. "A kitchen and a bathroom, too."

Dink noticed a yellow rubber dinghy strapped

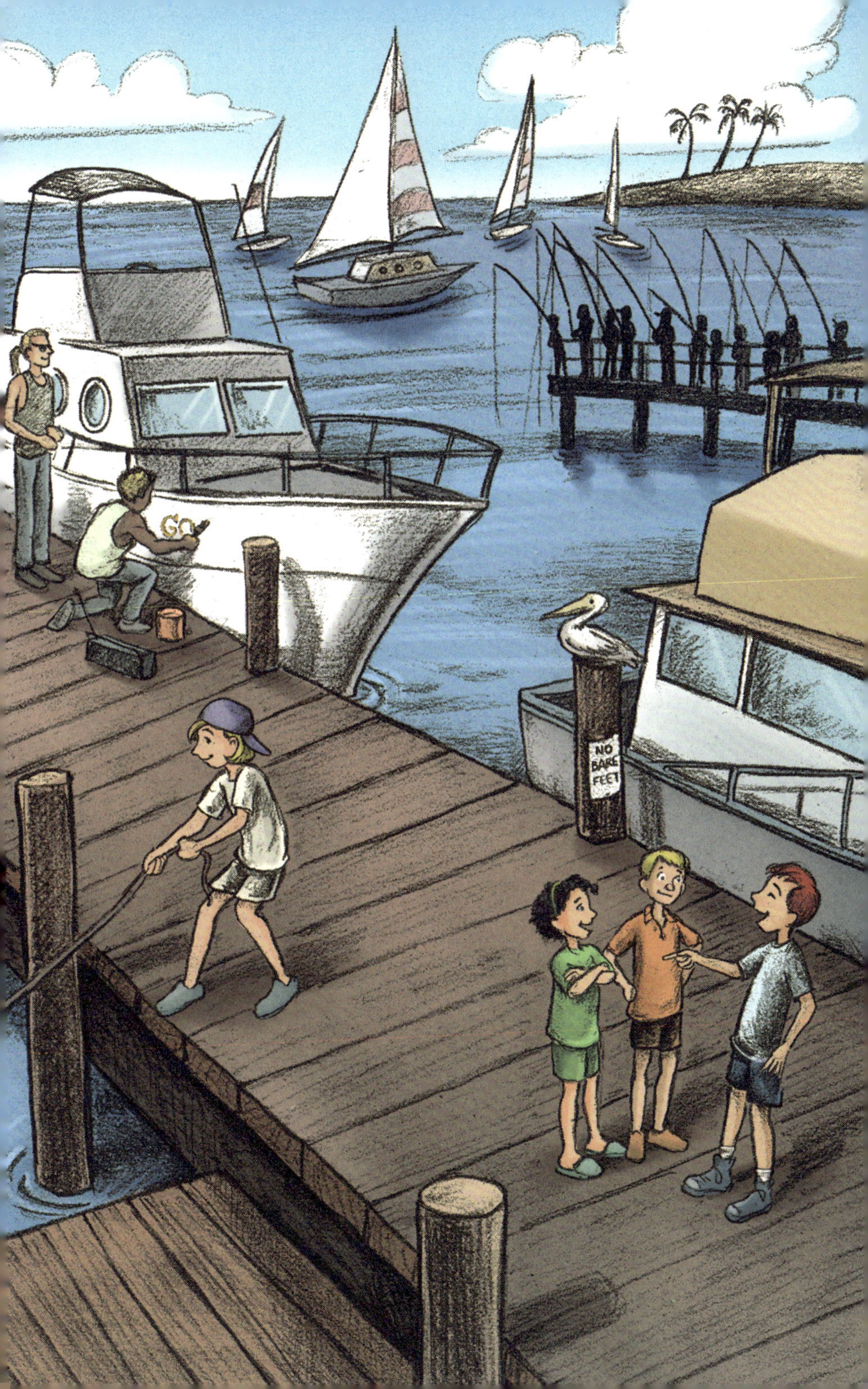
GO
NO BARE FEET

along one side of the boat. Two long fishing poles were lying on the deck.

"Is it a fishing boat?" Dink asked.

The skinny man shook his head. "Naw, we're after treasure. We dive for gold."

"You do?" Josh said. "Cool!"

The man waved his muffin out at the ocean. "There're plenty of sunken ships out there," he said, grinning. "Me and Spike here found one."

The man with the paintbrush gave his friend a sharp look. "Chip, maybe these kids don't want to know our business," he said.

Chip shrugged. "Just bein' neighborly," he said.

Spike went back to his painting.

"Did you find any gold yet?" Josh asked.

Chip looked at Spike.

"Yeah, we got some," Spike said.

"Could we see it?" Ruth Rose asked.

Spike thought for a minute, then handed Chip his paintbrush. "Sure, why not?" he said. "Come aboard and watch your feet."

Spike climbed down some stairs to a little cabin.

When he came back up, he had something shiny in his hand.

"These are Spanish coins," Spike told the kids. "Almost four hundred years old."

The kids stared at the gold coins in Spike's hand.

"Pretty neat, huh?" he asked.

The large gold coins gleamed in the sun.

"Awesome!" Josh said.

Chapter 3

The kids thanked Spike and Chip and walked back along the dock.

"I wonder how much those coins are worth," Josh said.

"A lot!" Ruth Rose said.

Josh sighed. "Wouldn't it be cool to dive for treasure?"

"Josh," Dink said, "you need to know how to use

an air tank and everything. They go down deep!"

Across the street, a small orange train was loading up with passengers.

"There's the trolley!" Ruth Rose said. "Let's catch it!"

The kids rushed over. They climbed aboard and sat right behind the driver. When most of the seats were filled, the trolley gave a jolt, then moved down the street.

"Where does the trolley go?" Dink asked the driver.

"We go everywhere, my man!" said the driver. He handed Dink a map. "See those blue circles? Those are my stoops. You can get off at any of them, then hop back on when I come by again."

The driver stopped the train in front of a white building with overflowing flower boxes. The sign in front of the building read MEL FISHER'S TREASURE MUSEUM. SEE SPANISH GOLD AND SILVER INSIDE.

"Who's Mel Fisher?" Dink asked the driver.

"Mel Fisher found an old Spanish ship loaded

with gold and silver," he said. "Some of what he found is in this museum."

He pointed at the sign. "Why don't you kids hop off and check it out? I'll swing by again in about forty-five minutes."

"All right!" Josh said.

The kids got off the trolley and followed a few of the other sightseers to the museum.

Inside were rows of glass cases. Each case held gleaming gold, silver, or jewelry.

The kids walked around the room staring at the priceless treasures.

After a while, Ruth Rose stopped in front of a picture of Mel Fisher. He was wearing a long gold

金鹅号的宝藏

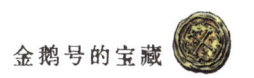

chain. The real chain was displayed in a glass case below the picture.

"Listen," Ruth Rose said. "'This solid gold chain was made in 1622 and weighs 200 pounds. It is worth more than one million dollars!'"

"Boy, imagine wearing that around your neck!" Josh said.

Dink was looking at a picture of Mel Fisher's boat. "Look, this says it took him almost twenty years to find the treasure!"

"Speaking of food, let's get some lunch," Josh said.

"We weren't talking about food," Ruth Rose said.

"Well, my stomach was," said Josh. "Looking at treasure makes me hungry!"

A few minutes later, the trolley stopped back at the museum.

"What'd you think of all that gold?" the driver asked them. "Pretty amazing, huh?"

"Did Mel Fisher get to keep everything he found?" Dink asked.

The driver shook his head. "Some had to go to the state of Florida, but he and his investors got rich on the rest."

"What're investors?" Josh asked.

"People who lent Mel Fisher money," said the driver. "Fisher had to borrow a lot to buy equipment and pay his crew. When he struck it rich, he paid his investors back with gold!"

The man grinned in his mirror. "Wish he'd asked me to invest!"

A few minutes later the kids said good-bye and hopped off the trolley. They raced home and rushed into Gram Hathaway's kitchen.

"How was your morning?" she asked.

"We rode on the trolley, Gram!" Ruth Rose said. "The driver was so nice!"

"He dropped us off at the Mel Fisher museum," Dink said.

"And we met two guys who dive for treasure," Josh added. "We went on their boat and saw real gold coins!"

Ruth Rose's grandmother smiled. "I'm glad you got to see some treasure," she said with sparkling eyes. "Now let me tell you about our special company! Their names are Spike and Chip."

Chapter 4

"Gram, how do you know Spike and Chip?" Ruth Rose asked.

"Wash up for lunch, and I'll tell you all about it," her grandmother said.

The kids crowded around the kitchen sink and washed their hands.

"A few weeks ago, Spike and Chip came to my senior center," Ruth Rose's gram said. She set a plate of sandwiches on the table.

The kids wiped their hands and sat down.

"They told us all about the treasure they found!" Gram continued. She poured lemonade. "Now they're looking for investors."

"Just like Mel Fisher!" Dink said. He reached for a tuna sandwich.

"That's right, Dink," Gram said.

Josh heaped three sandwiches onto his plate. "Are you gonna get rich?" he asked.

Ruth Rose's grandmother laughed. "We'll have to wait and see," she said. "Anyway, we're each thinking about investing ten thousand dollars!"

"Gram!" Ruth Rose said.

Her grandmother's eyes twinkled. "I know, it is a little scary."

"Boy, I'd do anything to go with them when they dive for treasure!" Josh said.

"That reminds me," Gram said. She took three presents off the counter. "Merry Christmas!"

"Wow, thanks, Gram!" said Ruth Rose.

"Yeah, thanks!" said Dink and Josh.

"They're all the same," Gram Hathaway said. "That way you won't have to share."

The kids pulled off the paper.

Inside, they each found a book called *Finding Sunken Treasure in Florida*.

The cover showed a boat like the one Mel Fisher had used. Under the boat was a sunken ship. Divers were searching the wreck and bringing up treasure.

"I thought you'd have fun learning about shipwrecks," said Gram, "since I might be investing in one!"

"This is so neat!" Josh said. "Thanks a lot!"

Ruth Rose's grandmother stood up. "You're very welcome. Now I have to get busy. Spike and Chip will be here in an hour! Can you help me set up the living room?"

"Sure," Dink said. "What do you want us to do?"

"I'll need about ten folding chairs. They're in the hall closet. And bring out the three card tables."

The kids arranged the tables and chairs around the living room. Gram Hathaway set out covered plates of cookies on one of the tables.

"Can we stay for the meeting?" Ruth Rose asked.

"Of course!" her grandmother said. "After you read those books, I expect you to ask intelligent questions!"

The kids took their books out to the front porch.

"Look," Josh said. "There's a whole chapter just about Mel Fisher."

Ruth Rose pointed to a map showing sunken ships. "They're all off the coast of Florida," she said. "If each one has treasure on it, think how much that is!"

Josh lay back on the porch and closed his eyes. "I'm staying here when you guys go back home. I'm gonna become a treasure hunter!"

Dink laughed. "You find treasure? You couldn't find your shorts this morning, Josh!"

Josh jabbed Dink with his knee. "Call me Captain Josh, please!"

Just then, a car pulled up. Two gray-haired women climbed out and hurried toward the house.

"I'm going in to help Gram," Ruth Rose said.

"We'll help, too," said Dink. He nudged Josh. "Come on, Captain Josh!"

Before they could go inside, a yellow cab stopped

A to Z 神秘案件

out front. Spike and Chip climbed out. Spike was carrying a wooden box. They were both dressed in clean pants, pressed shirts, and sandals.

"Hi!" Josh said as the two men walked up the sidewalk.

Spike and Chip stared at the kids. Finally, Chip waved. "How're you doing? Do you guys live around here?"

金鹅号的宝藏

Ruth Rose laughed. "No. We're visiting my grandmother. This is her house!"

Spike smiled. "What a small world," he said.

"Can I carry the box in?" Josh asked.

Spike shrugged. "It's pretty heavy."

"I can help," Dink said. They ran down the sidewalk, and Spike handed them the box.

Josh grinned as they lugged the heavy box up the steps. "My fingers feel all tingly!" he said.

Chapter 5

Gram Hathaway's living room was crowded with people. Spike and Chip sat at a small table with the box in front of them. Dink, Josh, and Ruth Rose perched on the stairs.

"Thank you all for coming!" Gram told everyone. Then she smiled at Spike. He stood up.

"Thanks for inviting us," Spike said. "Chip and I have been diving for a few years now. A couple weeks ago, we found a sunken ship."

Chip opened the box. Spike reached in and pulled out a gold cross, about eight inches tall. The gold shone warmly in the sunny room.

Someone said, "Oh, my goodness!" Spike gently laid the cross on the table.

Next he brought out a shiny hunk of silver, about the size of a big bar of soap. Then he spread a handful of gold coins on the table.

"There's a lot more down there," he continued. "We've found chains, silver goblets, even jewelry."

Gram's friends got out of their seats and crowded around Spike and Chip.

"May we touch it?" one woman asked.

Spike laughed. "Can't hurt it, ma'am. It's been on the bottom of the ocean for almost four hundred years!"

Josh was standing up so he could see. Gram Hathaway's friends were passing around the gold and silver.

"Um, Spike?" Josh said. "How did you get it so clean? Wouldn't it have barnacles and stuff all over it?"

Spike grinned. "Good question," he said. "First we soak the pieces, then we rub them with regular old vinegar. You'd be surprised how easily it cleans up."

Ruth Rose's hand shot up. "Can I ask a question?"

Spike nodded. "Ask away."

"It took Mel Fisher twenty years to find his sunken ship," said Ruth Rose. "How did you find yours so quickly?"

Spike smiled. "I guess we were just lucky," he said.

"And we had good maps," Chip added.

Spike turned back to the group. "I hope you'll all consider investing with us," he said. "Once we can buy some more equipment, we'll start bringing up some serious treasure."

Ruth Rose's grandmother stood up. "Why don't we have refreshments now?" she said.

Everyone began talking and filling small plates with cookies. Ruth Rose went into the kitchen for the lemonade.

Dink and Josh stayed on the stairs, near the table of goodies.

Spike and Chip stepped over to the refreshment table. Dink watched Spike take a few cookies.

"These cookies are loaded with chocolate chips," Spike whispered to his friend.

Dink was about to say something to Spike, but he stopped. He knew he had heard those words before!

Dink closed his eyes and tried to remember the voice he'd overheard in the airport. Dink was positive the man had said "...those cookies are loaded."

125

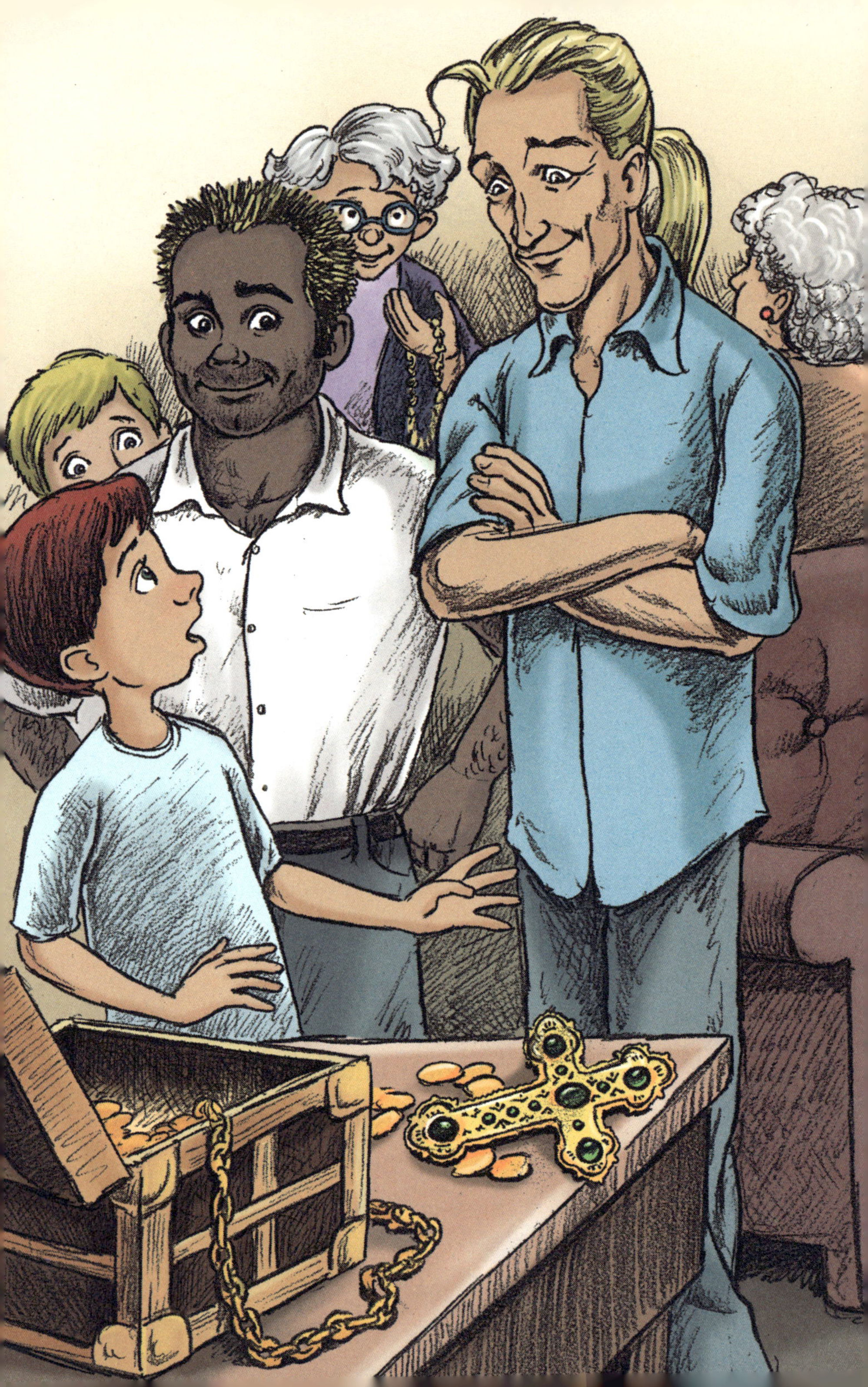

Dink was almost sure it had been the same voice!

He looked down for a tattoo, but Spike's pants covered his ankles.

The sandals looked the same. But a lot of people in Florida wore brown leather sandals.

"What's the matter?" Ruth Rose asked Dink. "You look like you smelled something rotten."

Dink stood up. "Come outside," he whispered. "It's important!"

Chapter 6

Josh and Ruth Rose followed Dink through the living room to the porch. They sat on the front steps.

"What's going on?" Josh asked. "I wasn't through with those cookies!"

"Remember the guy I told you about at the airport yesterday?" Dink asked. "Talking on the phone?"

Ruth Rose grinned. "Yeah, the cook you thought was planning a robbery."

Dink turned around and looked through the screen door. "I think it was Spike!"

Josh and Ruth Rose just stared at Dink.

Finally, Josh said, "What are you talking about, Dinkus?"

"I recognized his voice!" Dink said. "The guy at the airport said the same thing, that some old cookies were loaded."

Josh shook his head. "So?"

"Don't you see?" Dink said. "Maybe he meant Gram Hathaway's friends are loaded—loaded with money!"

Suddenly, the door opened, and Gram's friends began coming out. They all seemed excited about investing with Spike and Chip.

Then Spike and Chip came out carrying the box of gold. Gram Hathaway followed them onto the porch.

"Thanks for calling us a cab, Mrs. Hathaway," Spike said. "Do you really think your friends will help us out?"

Gram Hathaway smiled. "I wouldn't be a bit

surprised. I'm going to talk to my banker on Monday morning!"

A yellow cab pulled up, and Spike and Chip climbed in with the box. They waved out the window as the cab sped away.

"Wasn't that fun!" Ruth Rose's grandmother said. She stepped back into the house. "There are plenty of goodies left if anyone is hungry!" she called through the screen door.

"Thanks, Gram!" Ruth Rose said.

"She's pretty excited," she added after her grandmother had gone inside.

"I would be, too, if I was gonna get rich," Josh said.

Dink stood up. "Well, I don't think she's gonna get rich," he said. "I think she's gonna get robbed!"

"ROBBED!" Ruth Rose yelled.

"Yeah," Dink said. "Spike and Chip could just take off with your grandmother's money."

"But what about all that gold they just showed us?" Josh asked.

Dink shook his head. "I don't know about that,

but I do know what I heard."

"You know what you thought you heard," Josh said. "Besides, you don't know it was Spike. You never saw the guy on the phone."

"But I did see his feet!" Dink said. He told Josh and Ruth Rose about the tattoo he'd seen on the man's ankle.

"It's a good thing I'm such an observant young man," Josh said. "I know how we can settle this whole thing."

"How?" Ruth Rose asked.

"By finding out if it really was Spike that Dink heard on the phone."

Dink looked at him. "And how do we do that, oh observant one?"

Josh grinned. "Easy. We get Spike to show us his tattoo!"

Chapter 7

"Good idea," Dink said. "Let's go to the dock."

"Hold on," Ruth Rose said. She opened the screen door, grabbed some towels, and yelled, "GRAM, WE'RE GOING TO THE BEACH!"

Ruth Rose tossed towels to Dink and Josh as they walked down the sidewalk. "What if Spike's still wearing long pants?" she asked.

"Dink will think of something," Josh said. He

grinned at Dink. "Right?"

Dink shook his head. "This was your idea. Besides, you're the observant one!"

They thought about it as they walked. When they reached the boat dock, they still hadn't figured out what to do.

"I know," Josh said. "I'll tell him Dink is thinking of getting a tattoo! Then Spike will show us his!"

Dink laughed. "Kids can't get tattoos, Josh," he said.

A few moments later, the kids reached Spike and Chip's boat slip. But the boat wasn't there.

"They're gone!" Ruth Rose said.

"Now what?" Dink asked. "Should we wait till they come back in?"

"Why don't we hang out at the beach for a while?" Josh suggested. "That way, we can have fun and watch for the boat at the same time."

"Okay," Ruth Rose said. "But we can't stay out late. Gram will worry."

"Last one in kisses pelicans!" Josh yelled. He thundered down the dock and leaped onto the beach.

The kids swam, searched for shells, and buried Josh in the sand. By five o' clock, their skin was itchy with sunburn and salt.

"Look, isn't that their boat?" Ruth Rose asked.

A white boat was pulling in at the end of the dock.

"I think it is!" Josh said. "Come on!" The kids ran back along the dock.

They reached the boat as Chip was securing the lines. Spike was behind the wheel, just shutting down the motor.

Both men were wearing T-shirts and jeans. Spike's ankles were covered.

"Did you go diving?" Josh asked.

"We dive every day," Spike said, stepping onto the dock. He patted his stomach. "Right now, I need a couple of burgers. Ready, Chip?"

The kids walked with Spike and Chip to the end of the dock and said good-bye.

"We still didn't see a tattoo," Ruth Rose said as they headed for her grandmother's house.

"No, but I saw something else," Dink said. "They finished painting the name of the boat. It's the *Golden*

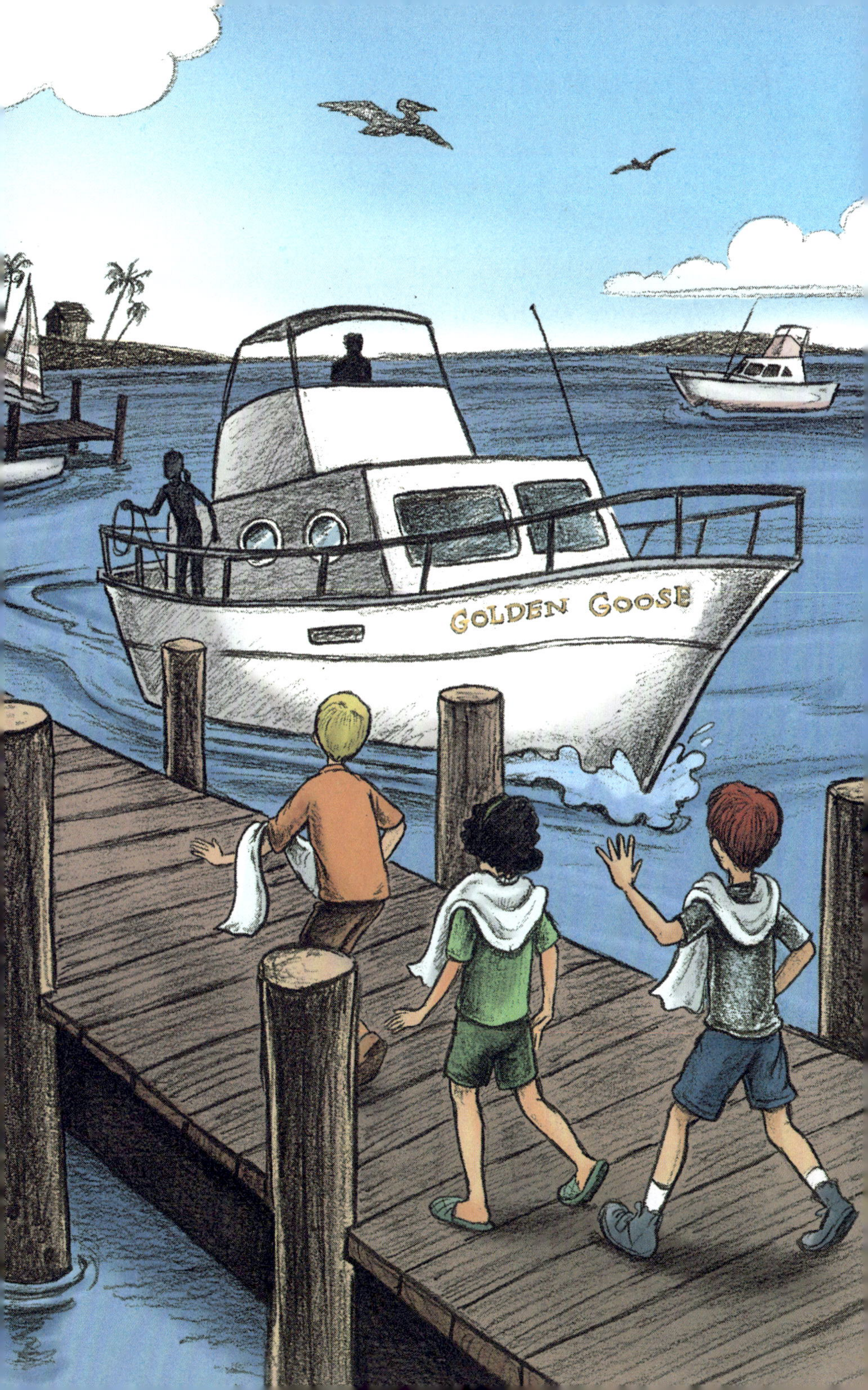
GOLDEN GOOSE

Goose."

Josh looked at him. "So?"

"The guy at the airport said something about drowning a goose," Dink said. "Maybe that's the goose he was talking about!"

"But what does it mean?" Ruth Rose asked. "Boats don't drown."

Dink shook his head. "I don't know."

A few minutes later, they saw Ruth Rose's grandmother. She was weeding in her front garden.

"Hi, Gram!" Ruth Rose called.

She looked up and waved.

"Tomorrow we go back to the boat and try again," Dink said, keeping his voice low. "You guys with me?"

"What if Spike's still wearing long pants?" Ruth Rose asked.

"Then I put my plan to work," Dink said.

"What plan?" Josh asked.

"I tell him about the tattoo contest," said Dink.

Josh stared at Dink. "What contest?"

"The one I just thought up," Dink said, tapping his head. "I'm gonna hang a poster down by the dock.

The poster will announce a tattoo contest. Then I'll tell Spike and Chip about the contest. If Spike has a tattoo on his ankle, he might mention it, or even show it to us."

"Dinkus was in the sun too long," Josh whispered loudly to Ruth Rose.

"I think it's brilliant!" Ruth Rose said. "Come on, I'll ask Gram for paper and markers!"

Chapter 8

Dink jumped out of bed. He shook Josh by the shoulder. "Josh, get up! We're going back to the dock!"

Josh opened one eye. "Time izzit?" he asked sleepily.

Dink glanced at the clock next to his bed. "Almost eight. Hurry up!"

Dink dressed in shorts and a T-shirt. He washed, brushed his hair, and grabbed the poster he'd drawn the night before.

"Come on, Josh!" he said, hurrying downstairs.

Ruth Rose was sitting at the table, spreading peanut butter on a bagel.

"Gram's out for her morning swim," she said. She pushed the plate of bagels toward Dink. "Where's Josh?"

Dink sat down and reached for the strawberry jam. "Still waking up," he said.

Dink unrolled the poster as Josh stumbled into the kitchen. His red hair was sticking straight up. "This plan had better work," he said. "I was dreaming I was King Midas. Only everything I touched turned to chocolate!"

Josh got a bagel and read Dink's poster through sleepy eyes. At the bottom Dink had drawn a man's arm with a tattoo of an owl.

> COME ONE, COME ALL!
> TATTOO CONTEST
> ON THE PIER
> Sunday night at 8:00
> CASH PRIZES FOR THE
> MOST CREATIVE TATTOOS.

"What happens when a bunch of people with tattoos show up, and there's no contest?" Josh asked.

Dink shrugged. "We have to find out if Spike has that tattoo on his ankle. Can you think of another way?"

140

Josh just shrugged.

"All right, then. Let's get going," Dink said.

They each grabbed an apple and headed for the dock. Dink carried the poster and four thumbtacks.

Even this early, people were strolling along the concrete pier. Dink tacked the poster to a light pole.

"Okay, now let's go find Spike and Chip," he said. They hurried to the dock.

A few people were on their boats, drinking coffee and enjoying the morning sun. The *Golden Goose* was tied at its slip.

Not a sound came from the boat.

"Think they're still asleep?" Josh asked.

Dink shrugged. "I don't hear any snoring."

Ruth Rose peered through one of the round cabin windows. "Nobody's down there," she said.

"Look, the door's open," Josh said. "They must be here."

Dink stepped onto the boat deck and knocked on the wood. "Hello?" he called. "Anyone home?"

Dink hopped back onto the dock. "Maybe they went out for breakfast," he said. "Let's wait."

The kids sat in the sun. A pelican waddled along the dock, stopping at each of the boats. A woman tossed him some bread.

Josh pulled his book out and began reading.

"Listen to this," he said. "'No matter how long it has been on the bottom of the ocean, gold stays shiny. But silver requires several days in a special chemical solution before it looks shiny again.'"

Josh looked up. "Yesterday, Spike told everyone they cleaned the gold and silver with vinegar!"

The kids looked at each other.

Dink got up and stepped aboard the *Golden Goose*. He walked around the deck, looking at everything and peeking into corners.

He stopped near an oxygen tank propped against a bench, then came back to the dock.

"That tank's empty," he told Josh and Ruth Rose.

"How do you know?" Josh asked.

"There's a round window with a dial," Dink said. "The little arrow is pointing to E."

"So maybe they used up all the oxygen and haven't filled it up yet."

"Maybe," Dink said. "But I don't see any other diving equipment."

Ruth Rose stepped closer to the deck. "Maybe they keep it down below," she said. She looked at the guys. "I say we check it out."

"Me too," Dink said.

Josh glanced back toward the pier. "What if they come back and catch us snooping?" he said.

"We'll tell them my grandmother sent us," Ruth Rose said. "I'll say she wants to ask them more questions."

"I think they hang pirates," Josh said.

"Josh, just looking on someone's boat doesn't make us pirates," Ruth Rose said. "If they're trying to cheat my grandmother, I'm gonna find out! Come on, we won't touch anything, we'll just look around."

She hopped aboard the boat and scooted down the cabin stairs. Josh and Dink followed.

The three stood in the middle of the small cabin. "What a smell!" Ruth Rose said.

"They aren't very neat, are they?" Josh said. The beds were unmade, and the tiny kitchen was a jumble of dirty dishes and glasses. The small eating table was covered with sticky-looking stains.

Dink glanced into a few dark corners. "I still don't see— "

"Shh! I heard something!" Ruth Rose said. She pointed above their heads. Suddenly, they all heard footsteps.

The kids looked at each other, wide-eyed.

Josh's face was white.

Dink looked around the small cabin, then rushed

金鹅号的宝藏

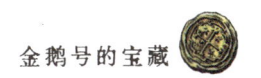

toward a narrow door in the back.

He yanked the door open and motioned for Josh and Ruth Rose to follow.

Chapter 9

The kids found themselves crammed in the boat's tiny bathroom.

There was no room to sit or turn around. The kids just stood and stared at each other.

Suddenly, they heard heavy feet thunder down the cabin stairs. They held their breath.

They heard a small thump, then a bigger one. Then the feet were walking again, this time going up the stairs.

The small room got hot fast. Sweat ran into Dink's eyes. He could barely breathe.

They waited, but heard no more noises.

"I smell scrambled eggs!" Josh whispered into Dink's ear.

Dink rolled his eyes.

"Well, I do!" said Josh.

Dink waited a few more minutes, then opened the door a crack. Cool air rushed into the bathroom.

Dink quickly looked around the cabin. He could hear the men talking up above. He gently pulled the door shut.

"They're up on deck," he said. "We can't stay in this bathroom. If one of them wants to use it, we're sunk!"

"Why don't we just leave?" Josh asked.

"How do we explain why we're hiding in their boat?" Ruth Rose said. "It's too late!"

Dink slipped out of the bathroom and saw a trapdoor in the floor.

Kneeling, Dink pulled the trapdoor open. Josh

and Ruth Rose tiptoed out of the bathroom.

Suddenly, the kids heard a roar. Then Dink felt the boat begin to move—backward!

"They're taking the boat out!" he whispered. "Come on, down here!"

The kids scampered down into the boat's hold. Dink lowered the door over their heads. Except for a crack of light around the trapdoor, they were in darkness.

"This place stinks like rotten fish!" Josh said.

"Now what?" Ruth Rose said.

"I don't know," Dink answered. He thought for a minute.

"They must be going out to the dive site," he said. "We'll have to hide till they decide to go back to the dock."

"But that could be all day!" Josh said.

The kids squirmed around, trying to get comfortable.

Dink put his eye up to the crack and saw the underside of the table. To the right, he could just make out the bottom stair leading up to the deck.

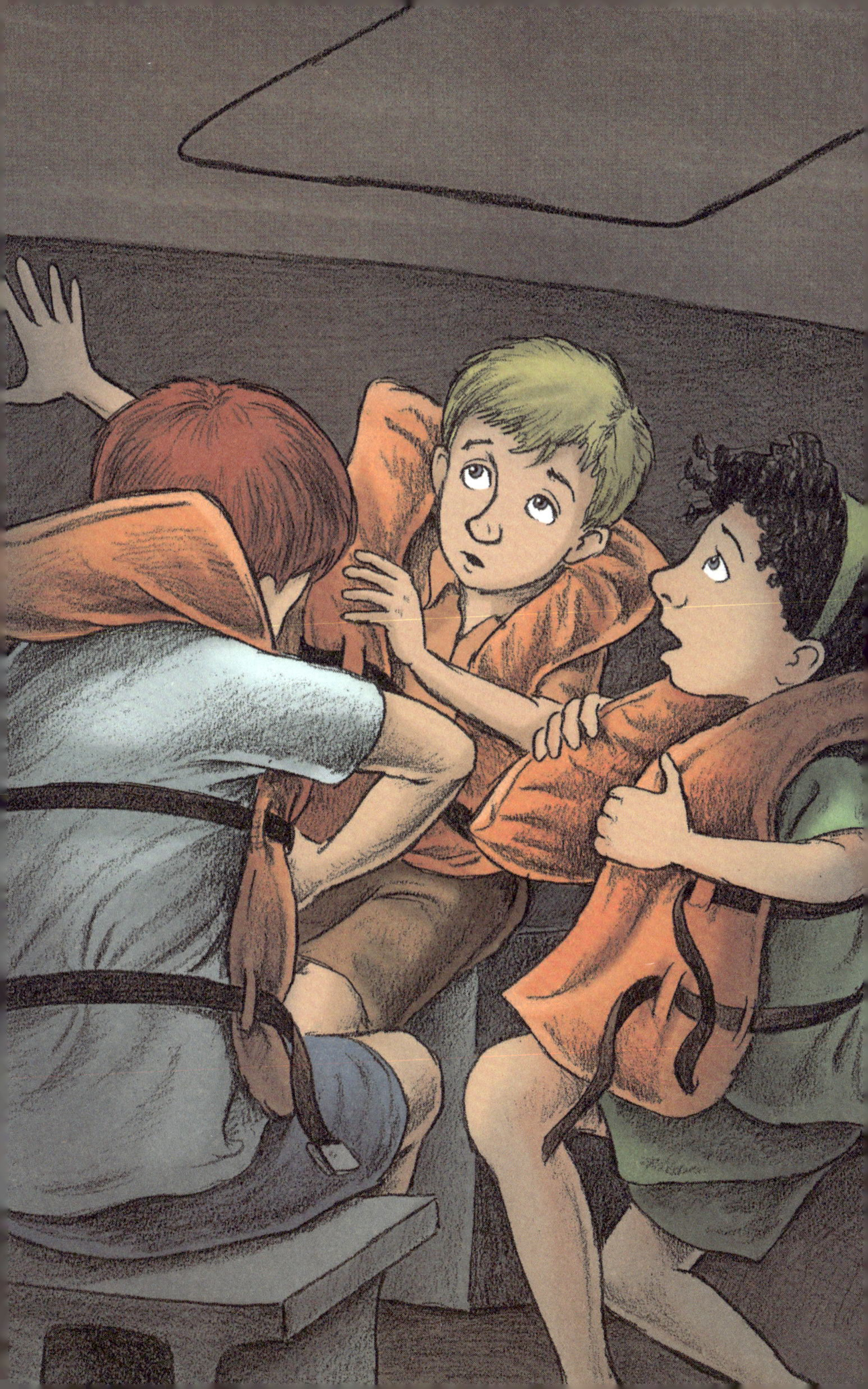

"Ouch!" Josh said suddenly. "I think I sat on an anchor!"

"And I scraped my knee on a cinder block!" Ruth Rose said.

Dink moved his hands around the sloping wooden floor. His fingers felt hard, scratchy surfaces. More cinder blocks, a bunch of them.

Then he touched something squishy.

"Guys, I found some life vests," Dink whispered. "Put 'em on!"

The kids struggled into the vests. Dink kept his eye on the crack. He wanted to know if Spike or Chip came down into the cabin.

"Whose idea was it to get on this boat?" Josh said. "I feel like a prisoner!"

"You wanted to go out on a dive," Dink said. "You got your wish!"

"Yeah," Josh said. "But not trapped in some smelly dungeon!"

Dink saw a movement through the crack. A pair of bare feet were backing down the stairs!

"Shh!" he said. "They're coming down to the

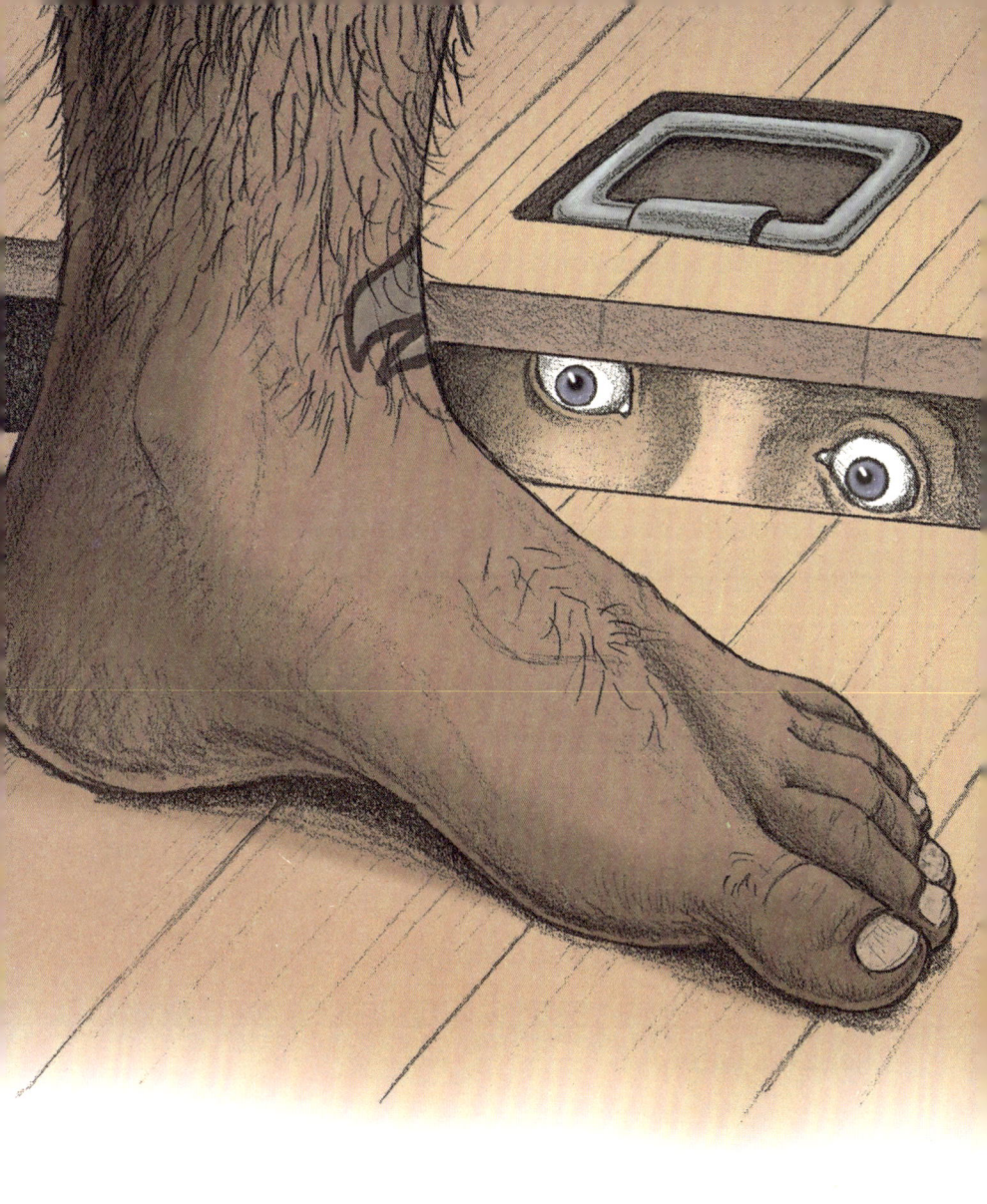

cabin!"

They heard footsteps, then voices. Shapes moved back and forth across the trapdoor.

"This place is a pigpen," one of the men said. Dink

151

recognized Spike's voice.

"Why bother to clean it?" Chip answered. He giggled. "It'll get real clean in a little while."

Dink heard something scrape, then a thump right over his head.

Through the crack, he saw skinny wooden legs. A stool or chair had been dragged up to the small table.

"We got any juice?" Spike asked.

"I doubt it," Chip answered. "I think there's milk."

"They're eating breakfast!" Josh hissed into Dink's ear. "I told you I smelled eggs!"

Then somebody sat down at the table. Dink could see one person's leg from the knee down.

The leg was hairy and tanned.

Suddenly, Dink gasped. Just inches from his eyes, he saw a tattoo.

It was an eagle's head.

Chapter 10

Spike was the man he'd overheard at the airport!

Suddenly, Chip was talking. "Ya know," he said, "I'm gonna miss this old tub when it's gone."

"Not me," Spike answered. "When we get the dough from the old folks, I'm buying the hottest car in Florida. I'm sick of living like a sardine!"

"So when do you want to do it?" Chip asked.

"Soon as I finish eating," Spike said. "I'll even let

you have the pleasure of using the ax."

Dink heard Chip laugh. "With all those cinder blocks we brought aboard, the *Goose* will go down in ten seconds!"

"Yeah, it should," Spike said. "Don't forget the box. We don't want that to sink, too!"

Dink felt Josh grab his arm and squeeze. On his other side, Ruth Rose let out a small gasp.

Spike and Chip were planning to sink the *Golden Goose*!

"Don't worry," Chip was saying. "I already put the gold in the dinghy."

A chair scraped, and the tattooed ankle disappeared from Dink's sight.

"After we drown the *Goose*, we'll take the dinghy back to town," Spike said. "We'll lie low till we get the money from the old folks."

He laughed. "Then we disappear."

Dink felt his stomach sink. He heard more thumps and footsteps.

"Make sure you don't leave anything aboard with your name on it," Spike said. "Paper floats, you know."

金鹅号的宝藏

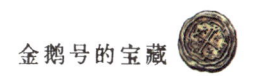

"Don't worry," Chip said. "Where's the ax?"

The voices faded away.

"Did you hear that?" Josh asked. "They're gonna sink this thing!"

"Shh!" Dink hissed. Suddenly, the kids heard loud smashing noises, one after the other.

Dink gulped. It was an ax striking wood!

Then he heard a thump and footsteps running up the cabin stairs.

Suddenly, he heard a new sound—the gurgle of water flooding into the boat!

"Now!" Dink said. He shoved the trapdoor open and scrambled out. Josh and Ruth Rose were right behind him.

They stepped into salt water.

"Look!" Ruth Rose pointed to a hole in the side of the cabin. Water was rushing in.

"What are we gonna do?" Josh asked.

Dink raced up the stairs and peeked. He saw Spike and Chip tearing across the water in the dinghy.

"They took

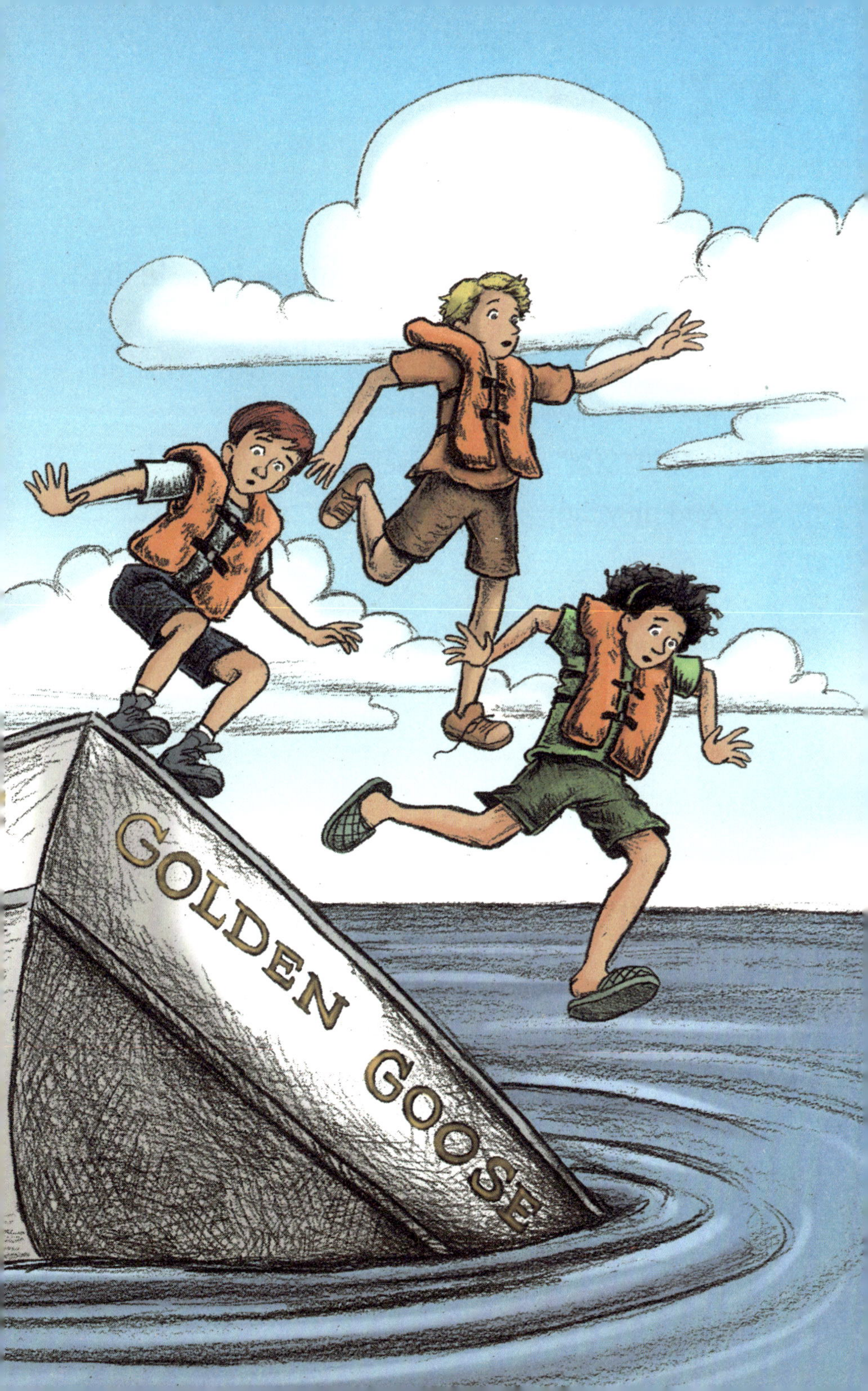
GOLDEN GOOSE

off!" Dink said. "Come on!"

The kids ran up the stairs and sprinted toward the rear of the boat.

Josh looked down into the water. "Now what do we do?" he squeaked.

"WE JUMP!" Ruth Rose yelled.

And they did.

Chapter 11

Dink felt the water rush over his head. Some got in his mouth before he remembered to shut it. His eyes stung from the salt.

Then his life vest shot him to the surface. He was floating.

Josh and Ruth Rose were bobbing nearby in their orange life vests.

"You guys okay?" Dink asked.

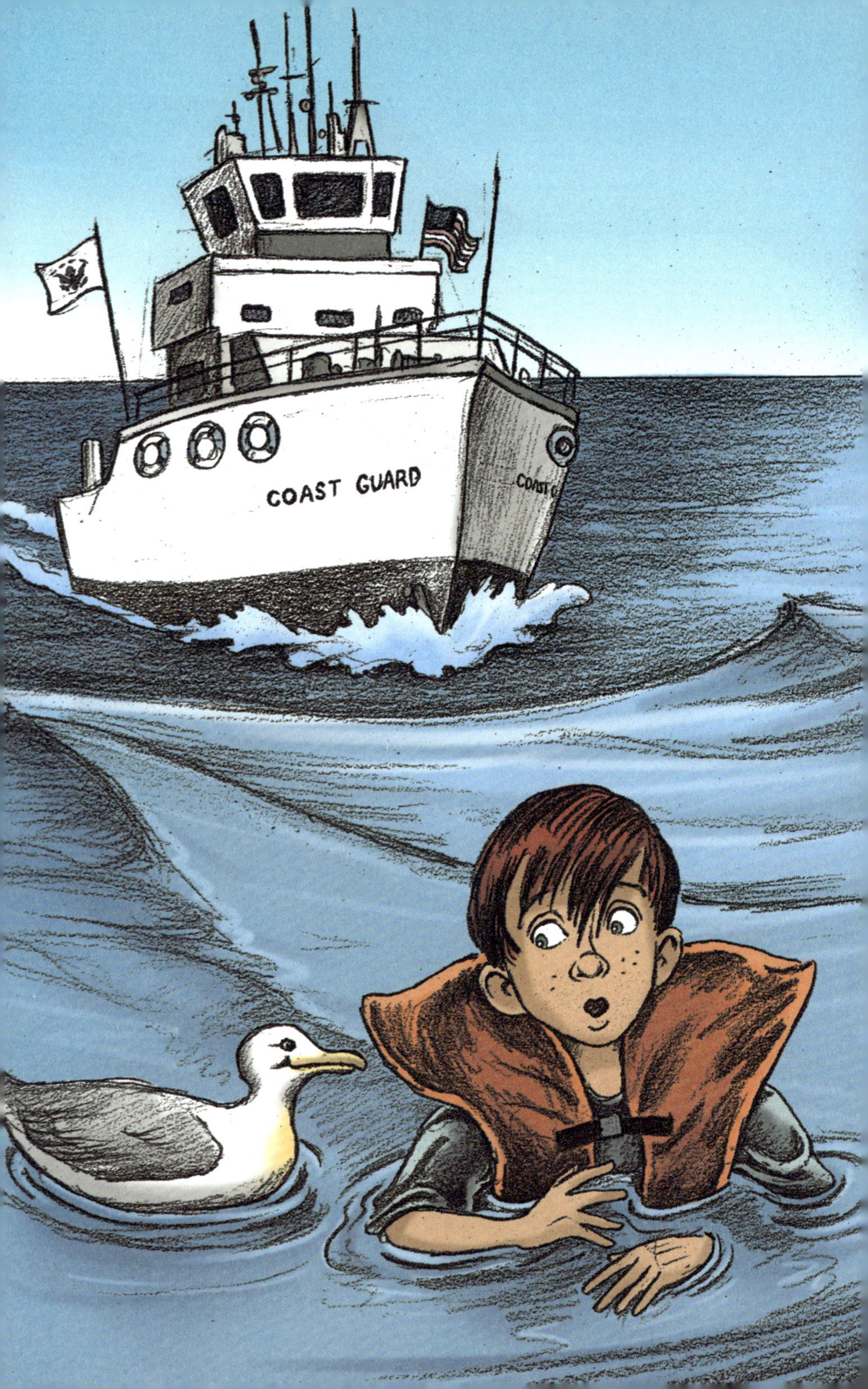
COAST GUARD

"Look!" Josh said, pointing at something over Dink's shoulder.

Dink spun around in the water.

The *Golden Goose* lay on its side. A few seconds later, it went under.

The kids heard a loud WHOOSH! as the boat disappeared.

"We got off just in time!" Josh said.

"Let's swim," Dink said. "Spike and Chip might decide to come back to make sure the boat sank!"

"Swim where?" Josh asked. "I can't even see land!"

"But I see some boats," Ruth Rose said, pointing one wet arm. "See those things sticking up out of the water?"

Josh began splashing his arms. "I think those are shark fins!" he yelled.

Ruth Rose laughed. "Sharks don't have white sails, Josh."

The kids began swimming toward the boats. Suddenly, Dink heard a roar.

He whipped his head around, expecting to see Spike and Chip bearing down on them. Instead, he saw a large white boat. On the side, in black letters, he read COAST GUARD.

The boat zoomed up, then slowed. The kids bounced in the waves like corks.

"What the heck are you kids doing!" a voice boomed from the boat.

Dink saw a man in a white uniform standing

on the deck. He was holding a bullhorn and glaring down at them.

Dink tried to yell, but a wave filled his mouth with water.

Another man threw three round life preservers into the water. "Hang on to those!" the man in white bellowed.

The rings splashed into the water only a few feet away.

Seconds later, Dink, Josh, and Ruth Rose were hauled onto the boat's deck.

The kids huddled together. A group of men stood staring at them.

The sun was warm, but Dink couldn't stop shaking.

One of the men draped blankets around their shoulders.

"Well?" the uniformed man said. "I'm waiting."

He stared at the kids with a strange expression on his face. "You do speak English, I hope."

Josh grinned. "Yeah. Do you guys have anything to eat? I'm starving!"

The men laughed.

The man holding the bullhorn grinned. "Okay, kids, first you tell us why you were swimming to Cuba," he said, "then we feed you!"

"Awesome!" Josh said as burst after burst of fireworks went off in the sky. It was ten o' clock on New Year's Eve, two days after they'd been rescued by the Coast Guard boat.

The kids were lying on the lawn in Gram's backyard. They had just finished a lobster dinner, and their stomachs were full.

Gram came out carrying a tray. "Who has room for chocolate ice cream?" she asked.

Dink groaned. "If I eat one more thing, I'll bust wide open!"

Josh sat up. "I'll have some!" he said.

Gram set the tray on the blanket. "Help yourself," she said, joining the kids.

"That was a super meal, Gram," Ruth Rose said.

"My pleasure!" Gram said. "You kids are heroes! Thanks to you, the police were able to catch Spike and

Chip. We almost lost a lot of money!"

"Well, Dinkus," Josh said, "you were right. It was Spike on the phone at the airport, and he did say, 'take the dough!' "

Gram Hathaway squeezed Dink's hand. "You saved the day!" she said.

Dink blushed. "Well, you guys helped, too," he said. "If it hadn't been for Ruth Rose, we wouldn't have been on the *Golden Goose* when those two guys came back. They'd have sunk the boat and gotten away with the money."

"And Josh figured out they were lying about how to clean gold and silver," Ruth Rose said. "I never even saw that in my book."

Gram Hathaway smiled. "I know three children who are going to get a reward," she said.

"A reward?" Josh said. "For what?"

"The gold and silver Spike and Chip showed us was stolen from a museum in Miami," Gram said. "The museum was offering a reward, and it goes to you three!"

"Awesome—how much?" Josh said.

Ruth Rose laughed. "Don't be greedy, Joshua."

Josh slurped up the last of his ice cream. "I'm not greedy," he said. "I just like money!"

Suddenly, a huge mushroom of fireworks went off over their heads. Red, blue, and green sprays of light cascaded toward the earth.

"Make a wish, everyone!" Gram said.

"I wish I had more ice cream," Josh said.

"I wish I had my own computer," Ruth Rose said.

"I wish we could stay here longer," Dink said. "Our vacation went by so fast!"

Gram Hathaway gave Dink a kiss on the cheek. "Your wish is granted," she said. "You're all invited back this summer!"

Text copyright © 1999 by Ron Roy
Cover art copyright © 2015 by Stephen Gilpin
Interior illustrations copyright © 1999 by John Steven Gurney
All rights reserved. Published in the United States by Random House Children's Books,
a division of Random House LLC, a Penguin Random House Company, New York.
Originally published in paperback by Random House Children's Books, New York, in 1999.

本书中英双语版由中南博集天卷文化传媒有限公司与企鹅兰登（北京）文化发展有限公司合作出版。

"企鹅"及其相关标识是企鹅兰登已经注册或尚未注册的商标。
未经允许，不得擅用。
封底凡无企鹅防伪标识者均属未经授权之非法版本。

©中南博集天卷文化传媒有限公司。本书版权受法律保护。未经权利人许可，任何人不得以任何方式使用本书包括正文、插图、封面、版式等任何部分内容，违者将受到法律制裁。

著作权合同登记号：字18-2023-258

图书在版编目（CIP）数据

金鹅号的宝藏：汉英对照 /（美）罗恩·罗伊著；
（美）约翰·史蒂文·格尼绘；叶雯熙译. -- 长沙：湖
南少年儿童出版社，2024.10. --（A to Z神秘案件）.
ISBN 978-7-5562-7817-6
Ⅰ. H319.4
中国国家版本馆CIP数据核字第2024KW6726号

A TO Z SHENMI ANJIAN JIN'E HAO DE BAOZANG

A to Z神秘案件 金鹅号的宝藏

[美] 罗恩·罗伊 著　　[美] 约翰·史蒂文·格尼 绘　　叶雯熙 译

责任编辑：唐 凌　李 炜	策划出品：李 炜　张苗苗　文赛峰
策划编辑：文赛峰	特约编辑：杜天梦
营销编辑：付 佳　杨 朔　周晓茜	封面设计：霍雨佳
版权支持：王媛媛	版式设计：马睿君
插图上色：河北传图文化	内文排版：马睿君

出 版 人：刘星保
出　　版：湖南少年儿童出版社
地　　址：湖南省长沙市晚报大道89号
邮　　编：410016
电　　话：0731-82196320
常年法律顾问：湖南崇民律师事务所　柳成柱律师
经　　销：新华书店
开　　本：875 mm×1230 mm　1/32
字　　数：94千字
版　　次：2024年10月第1版
书　　号：ISBN 978-7-5562-7817-6

印　　刷：三河市中晟雅豪印务有限公司
印　　张：5.25
印　　次：2024年10月第1次印刷
定　　价：280.00元（全10册）

若有质量问题，请致电质量监督电话：010-59096394　团购电话：010-59320018